THIS IS REALITY

Roy Eugene Davis is founder-director of Center for Spiritual Awareness, a New Era truth movement with an international outreach. He began his spiritual training with Paramahansa Yogananda in 1950. Mr. Davis is the editor-publisher of *Truth Journal* magazine, author of many inspirational books and a world-traveled teacher of meditation methods and how-to-live principles.

ROY EUGENE DAVIS
COLLECTED WRITINGS
Volume One

THIS IS REALITY

CSA PRESS, *Publishers*
Lakemont, Georgia 30552

*Copyright © 1962
by Roy Eugene Davis*

THIS EDITION 1983

This title is Volume One of the Collected Writings Series. Contact the Publisher for a complete list of other available titles by the author: CSA Press, Post Office Box 7, Lakemont, Georgia 30552. CSA Press is the literature department of Center for Spiritual Awareness.

MANUFACTURED IN THE UNITED STATES OF AMERICA

INTRODUCTION

If there is one handbook which is treasured by disciples on the spiritual path, because of its clear explanation of the nature of consciousness and the way to experience enlightenment, it is the *Yoga Sutras*. The word *sutra* means "thread" and it was the custom of ancient Vedic sages to write, in concise form, the essence of their realizations. The student was then to contemplate the meaning of the statements and awaken to his own personal realization.

Patanjali, the author of the *Yoga Sutras*, did not originate the science of yoga or the procedures and techniques. He restated, in orderly sequence, the teachings of enlightened yogis and seers. Yoga is for all times, all places and all people. Any person of any Faith and in any walk of life can practice meditation and apply the principles of mind and consciousness so well shared here.

This Is Reality was published in 1962 as a study manual for students and disciples. When released to the general reading public it became extremely popular and went through many editions in both the English and German versions. I withdrew the book from circulation after writing another commentary on the *Yoga Sutras* several years later, but the demand for it has continued. I am, therefore, pleased to once again offer *This Is Reality* in this new form.

We have had the original text reproduced, minus a section on techniques and procedures which appeared in the earlier version. Since we are engaged in reprinting a number of my titles, to be of standard size and format, this particular book has wider margins on the pages because of the use of the original type and layout.

For readers interested in continued and deeper study of the *Yoga Sutras* I recommend my more recent commentary, which is found in *The Science of Kriya Yoga* and published by CSA Press.

I first met my guru, Paramahansa Yogananda, in 1949. It is my hope that the reader will experience the spirit and consciousness of my guru line as a result of careful and reverent study of this text.

Roy Eugene Davis

Lakemont, Georgia
June 20, 1983

*I salute the supreme teacher, the Truth,
whose nature is bliss, who is the giver
of the highest happiness, who is pure
wisdom, who is beyond all qualities and
infinite like the sky, who is beyond words,
who is one and eternal, pure and still,
who is beyond all change and phenomena
and who is the silent witness to all our
thoughts and emotions—I salute Truth,
the supreme teacher.*

—Ancient Vedic Hymn

CONTENTS

INTRODUCTION

BOOK ONE
A Commentary on Concentration   15

BOOK TWO
The Practice of Concentration   45

BOOK THREE
Perfect Superconsciousness and Soul Ability   83

BOOK FOUR
Liberation   133

BOOK ONE

A Commentary on Concentration

A COMMENTARY ON CONCENTRATION

1. Concentration.

The most often emphasized, and the least understood word, is concentration. Too many times we confuse the word concentration, with the idea that we are to use will power and effort, to accomplish a given purpose. *Concentration is the act of directing the attention to one point.* This flowing of attention can be quite effortless, as long as there is a steady flow of attention and no diversion is allowed to interfere.

The secret of controlling life experience is tied up in the proper understanding of concentration. A man who knows how to concentrate, can accomplish more, in a few hours, than the average person can accomplish in many days or weeks. An enthusiastic man who is serious about coming to a point of illumination can, by controlled attention, shorten the time factor and accomplish his illumination in this lifetime, rather than take the arduous path of several lifetimes. The secret of self-liberation is in the hands of the person who knows the art of concentration.

2. Controlled Concentration Prevents the Formation of Mental Patterns.

While it is perfectly all right to form mental patterns, so as to direct the flow of this ever-moving Life Force into form for the purpose of taking dominion, or for the purpose of setting up a situation, for meditation we are concerned with preventing the mental patterns from forming, as this would only be an impediment to our practice. *It is not a matter of creating an inner experience by visualizing our concept of the Infinite, but it is a matter of releasing the desire to form mental patterns, so the awareness will be free of association and diversion.*

3. Perfection in the Practice of Concentration Enables the Practitioner to Experience the Absolute Reality.

As it is the identification with ideas, and manifestations of ideas, that causes man to feel that he is separate from Reality, then it is obvious that the removal of thought, and the proper identification being established, will enable him to cognize his own Self-Awareness, which is nothing more than the Omnipresent Awareness. The restless mental activity lashes creation into form as far as the individual is concerned, and his acceptance of creation as cause instead of effect, leads him to accept an erroneous concept, *thus his concept of life is an illusion, based upon a false premise.* When the mind reasons, even if the reasoning is perfect, if the data is incorrect, then the conclusion will be incorrect. So it is man's misunderstanding about himself as being a limited creature, that causes all the trouble. It is the purpose of this book to clear up this misunderstanding.

4. In Ordinary Consciousness Man Is Identified with His Mental Creations.

In the true sense everything that man might perceive is a product of his imagining. Just as his personal world is the result of his mental attitude, so his larger world is the result of collective acceptance. Though man in the true sense does not create anything, he simply beholds it, and has the ability to bring an already manifested form from one dimension to another, at will. When an adept appears to precipitate an object, he really brings the idea of the object from the idea realm and causes it to be stabilized on this dimension. This causes particles of dense substance of this dimension to form about the idea or pattern. So while it appears that something was created out of nothing, it is understood that the idea existed even though unmanifest on this level, and had but to be brought forth into expression. This seems to be a power, but it is really an ability to accept it as a possibility. The reason the average person cannot do it is because the average person is so convinced of the solidness and reality of this dimension, he cannot accept the fact that it is really fluid, and is easily formed by the mind of the supposed creator.

The entire list of man's problems, his troubles, limitations, psychic injuries, diminishing of energy, and eventual death to this world is the result of his misunderstanding.

5. For the Purpose of Clarification We Shall Discuss Five Classifications of the Mental Attitude.

If we are to understand the mental action, we must take a closer look at the process whereby Substance is formed by the individual, and collective mental attitude. The following six paragraphs will explain this process in detail.

(A) THE FIVE CLASSIFICATIONS ARE:

Direct or intuitive perception, indiscrimination, delusion, sleep, and memory. We will deal first with:

(B) DIRECT OR INTUITIVE PERCEPTION

The best way to know anything is to simply *know it*. This viewpoint is inconceivable to the person who is used to the process of trying to know by acquiring outside knowledge, or who prides himself on his accumulation of facts and figures, which in turn have been assembled by others by a like process. The best way to know is to *know*. And this is a faculty of the Soul or Unit of Awareness. Soul does not need to learn anything, though it does need to be conditioned in order to adapt to a specific environment. Meditation and pure concentration is the way to find release from conditioning when the need arises. The demonstrations of Soul power and related phenomena, such as clairvoyance, clairaudience, projection of awareness and one or a number of bodies, is due to the exercising of the Soul's ability to various degrees. We shall deal with this later in this commentary.

(C) INDISCRIMINATION

As we mentioned earlier, if we have incorrect data on hand, then our conclusions will be wrong regardless of how clear-headed we may be during the reasoning process. When we accept this world of form as the only reality and base all actions and premises on this belief, then we are not discriminating. We are not seeing the One Power behind the form. There is but One Power, and this One Power takes form on all levels, as Substance manifesting. It is incorrect to say that there is a Creator and creation. There is only the Creator and the Creator in form. Everything that the mind of man can behold, and conceive of beholding, is part and parcel of this One Consciousness. Belief in separation is the reason for indiscrimination and suffering.

(D) DELUSION

Self-delusion is possibly one of the most attractive diversions that an aspiring Soul can enter into. The process of awakening to the real and eternal vision, sometimes seems so far off (merely another instance of indiscrimination), that to avoid the seeming dryness of everyday effort, a person will often fabricate a picture of what he thinks the levels of pure awareness will be like, and projects them as wish-fulfillments. They will seem real for a while because of the intensity of desire that they be real, but soon will fade and the barren state of feeling will be a real letdown. Here is where we need self-honesty. I have yet to see a self-deluded person who really believed that he was what he claimed to be, for in his quiet moments the harsh reality would come to the surface. Self-deluded souls are evident in their attempt to masquerade and put on airs but, unfortunately, their superficial attitude is not enough to enable them to really demonstrate according to their supposed level of consciousness. Self-delusion is to be avoided and one of the best ways to avoid it is to keep the company of a Self-realized Soul or Preceptor, and to seriously consider the advice that such a person will give.

(E) SLEEP

In a certain sense, everyone who operates through a body on one level or another is *sleeping,* in that they are less aware than they could be. Man has to accept a certain limitation if he is to operate through a body. This is a self-imposed limitation and is released when the body is discarded. The ordinary sleeping process is largely a habit of the body. Man finds, in sleep, an opportunity to withdraw from contact with this world, and is refreshed. The proper understanding of sleep will enable a man to know who he really is. There are many techniques to practice so that the act of sleeping can be used as a gateway to unlimited expression. The average man uses sleep as an escape from harsh reality, but through the proper practice of meditation and pure concentration, he learns to abandon sleep entirely. *When he can do this, he has overcome death.*

(F) MEMORY

If a person endeavors to attain a measure of stability by remembering events or experiences of this life, or past lives, he is still in delusion. For all he will be recalling will be *pictures* which were accepted while he was under one or more levels of indiscrimination. We do not need proof that we existed, for the fact that we exist now is sufficient proof of that. What we need is realization of our nature, as unconditioned awareness. It is easy to recall any event or situation to which we have been exposed, for the *picture* is retained on some level of our being, by the very fact that we experienced it. The secret of perfect recall lies in our willingness to remember. Many times we cannot remember because we are afraid to take the responsibility of remembering. Or we are afraid that we cannot take the emotional pain that will attend the memory.

The real purpose of using memory is to remember back through the years and incarnations of semi-dream experiences and remember our *real* nature. We need not *attain* to any great state of consciousness; we need but to remember, or become aware of, our present great state.

6. One May Control the Mental Attitudes by Steady Practice and by the Proper Understanding of Non-attachment.

In order to practice properly one must have adequate instruction, and a knowledge of the mind, as well as the interaction of forces and energies. Through the techniques to be found in this manual, anyone of average ability who is serious about coming into the realization of pure consciousness may do so.

Non-attachment does not mean relinquishment of this or any other world, but it means the proper recognition of the One Consciousness working in and through all forms, as the forms, and as the activity. It means to release the little concept and embrace the cosmic viewpoint. Thus non-attachment means liberation into a greater sphere of expression.

7. It Is of Particular Importance to Understand Concentration and to Practice It.

The attention wanders from force of habit, but the steady-minded practitioner will always be sure to draw the attention back and expand the awareness. It is this necessity for steady application that gives the beginning student the impression of effort. But an active use of effort, which implies doubt, will defeat the purpose. It will usually be found that in states of advanced meditation the breathing of the physical body will be very slow, and the activities of the body will come practically to a standstill as the attention is withdrawn from the external world and thrown within. In fact, it is possible to induce certain states of mental quietude by properly understanding the action of the breath and body. A whole system of practice known as Yoga has been evolved to encompass this need, and the presentation here set forth will be found to be compatible with Yoga practice and with the practice of any similar system, as we are dealing with the science of the process.

8. Intense Belief in the Possibility of the Goal Being Accomplished Is of Primary Importance.

Many otherwise serious practitioners of this science will apply themselves faithfully to the letter of the practice, but will not have the inner conviction that they can attain. This is to be avoided at all costs, for it is true that we move forward into our psychological assumptions, *the acceptance being the door through which we pass.* This is different from the problem of the deluded person who projects his desire, for this is the process of accepting the Reality of the pure experience. It will be helpful in this direction to read the life experiences of others who have attained to certain states of consciousness, and thus by mental association acquire a feeling of the level of consciousness.

9. The Way to Liberation and Dominion Is to Be Non-attached to the Objects and Appearances of This World, Which Are Projections of Mind Activity.

Non-attachment is not withdrawal from life, but it is the state of recognition of the One Consciousness, pervading everything. With the realization of the One Consciousness, there is the release of compulsive desire, for there comes the automatic realization that everything is here and now, not to be attained or lost, but to be accepted. This is the fourth dimensional vision wherein we get the view of the permanency of things.

10. Perfect Understanding of Non-attachment Gives Complete Understanding of Life on All Levels.

When we cease running here and there to acquire knowledge, but instead learn to rest in the realization that everything is here and now if we can but perceive it, then we get over the idea that we have to develop, or learn, or grow, and we come to the understanding of our real nature, which is already perfect, free, and all-knowing.

11. Realization of Pure Consciousness or Superconsciousness Comes as a Result of Perfect Concentration and Meditation.

Understanding the basic law that man identifies with the object of his concentration, we see the futility of trying to attain superconsciousness by concentrating upon mundane things. Such concentration or direction of attention only makes us more solidly identified with the objects and qualities of this world. Perfect concentration (or flowing of attention) on the superconscious (unconditioned) state will bring the full awareness to the superconscious level.

12. **There Is a High Level of Superconsciousness Which Is Experienced as the Mental Activity Is Brought to a Standstill. However, in This Early Stage Even Though There Is a Stopping of External Mental Activity, There Is Still the Activity of the Inner Impressions.**

One of the early stages of Samadhi or Superconscious Awareness comes as a result of the mental activity being brought to a standstill. It is an erroneous conviction held by many that one has to think to be aware. The pure awareness needs no mental activity. In this level of pure awareness one knows, simply by knowing. Everything is self-revealed. The mental activity can be brought to a standstill in deep meditation, if one is willing to sit for a long period of time and let the restless body activity settle down. As the restlessness of body is overcome through deep relaxation, the mental activity will slow down; and as this happens, if the one who is meditating avoids sleep and becomes clearer in vision, then the conditioning of the mind is transcended and superconscious perception is experienced. Activity remains on the subtle levels of mind at this point, however, but will be resolved by deeper practice.

13. **When This State of Superconsciousness Is Attained, but the Individual Is Not Established in Perfect Non-attachment, Then This State of Consciousness Enables Him to Operate in This World in Magnificent Fashion, but He Does Not Transcend It.**

Because in this early stage, man has withdrawn from this world, but is not yet fully aware of his real nature, having only had a glimpse of it in the silence; because of his belief in the reality of this plane (because he has not attained pure vision or the understanding of the One Life everywhere present); he must be content to function on this plane. His ability to operate here, however, will be greatly increased because he will be operating from a higher level of awareness, and he will be able to see through some of the problems that beset ordinary man. At this stage of unfoldment it is very important that the motives be pure.

14. It Is Also Possible to Attain This Level of Perfect Superconsciousness Through Faith, Energy, Memory, Concentration, and Discrimination.

In the earlier paragraph we pointed out that perception of superconsciousness came about as we were able to shed the restriction of the restless mental activities, by a process of letting them settle down and by keeping our center of awareness. There are other approaches, however, and the aspiring individual should follow the path to which he is inclined. We shall deal with each path which leads to the realization of Samadhi or Perfect Superconsciousness.

(A) FAITH

To have faith means to have the perfect vision that the state desired is already established, and to so concentrate or believe, that it does emerge to the surface to be manifest. It is the recognition of Reality and the non-recognition of ideas contrary to it.

(B) Energy

If we are energetic we will let nothing stand in the way of our attainment and will keep right on with the process. It takes steady practice to keep the attention flowing in the right direction, but those who practice make rapid progress, as compared to others who waste time and allow the attention to be scattered in many different directions.

(C) Memory

As mentioned earlier in this text, if one will practice remembering back through the experiences of this and former lives, without getting lost in the maze of former experiences, then it is conceivable that one will pierce the veil of memory and be aware of the unconditioned state once more.

(D) Concentration

This is also described in detail in the early pages of this text.

(E) Discrimination

As indiscrimination leads to bondage, so discrimination, or the ability to see perfection in any and all situations, leads to the realization of Perfect Superconsciousness.

15. Individuals Who Are Ambitious Make Rapid Progress on the Path.

To maintain interest and enthusiasm we should make it a point to constantly remind ourselves of our real purpose in this life. Even though it appears that we have many responsibilities and obligations, we are wise to keep our eyes upon the goal at all times.

16. The Length of Time It Takes to Attain the Perfect Superconscious State Depends upon Whether the Practitioner Is Mild, Medium or Intense in Practice.

Many times a person will say, "How long will it take to attain?" The answer, of course, depends upon the time and creative effort that person is willing to spend for the purpose. Those who practice only mildly, just barely move ahead of the ordinary evolutionary pattern and speed of unfoldment. Those who are more enthusiastic naturally make faster progress because they spend more time living according to the principles. Persons who make the most rapid progress are the ones who are intense in their practice, though this is not to be confused with a sense of compulsive urgency, which is an indication of a deep feeling of lack and emptiness. A strong sense of "I have already attained" coupled with a bit of patience until it becomes so, is a good balance.

17. Perfect Superconsciousness Is Also Attained by Identifying with the Ultimate Reality or Absolute.

A dynamic realization of the perfect state of being, here and now, is known as the unshakeable attainment. In this realization the concepts, beliefs, and even subtle mental impressions of being anything but perfectly self-realized, are wiped away. There are some who are self-deluded on this point and this is evident in that they cannot operate from their supposed level of consciousness, but merely give excuses for their failure to do so. Hence, the value of having a close association with an honest and disinterested person with insight, who will point out this error.

18. **Perfect Superconsciousness (Identification with the Absolute) Is a Level of Awareness, Untouched by Unhappiness, Cause and Effect, or Compulsive Desire.**

When one is established in the realization of the Infinite, there can be no unhappiness because the viewpoint is above the idea of duality and there is awareness, but no fluctuation of consciousness. In this state of awareness, in the understanding of what life is all about, there is no need to be under the law of cause and effect. Since there is the realization of completeness, there is no compulsion. *This is the state of liberation.*

19. **In This Master Consciousness (Perfect Superconsciousness) There Is Complete Beingness, Whereas in the Individualized Manifestation or Soul Consciousness This Perfection Exists, but Is Not Wholly Manifest.**

We often see aspects of the Infinite, manifested in individuals who are making the attempt to extend the awareness; but in the person who rests in the complete realization, we see the individuality merged in the ocean of Life.

20. **This Master Consciousness, Being Free of the Qualifications of Time, Is the Only Teacher, Ancient or Modern.**

Though it may appear that there are various grades of Teachers, Masters, or Adepts to the eye of the uninitiated, in reality there is but one Teacher, as there is but one Life. Teachers, Masters, Adepts and Preceptors are manifestations of the Life and act as points of contact through which the power can flow into expression on various levels. The right Teacher will always be at that point in time and space when it is necessary for the student to have the contact. Life takes care of itself and with this realization, the sincere aspirant has only to envision ever higher and higher steps on the ladder of unfoldment, knowing that the right experience will meet him every step of the way.

21. **The First Obvious Manifestation of Consciousness on the Three Dimensional Level Is Recognized as the Atoms Vibrating. This Vibration, Heard Intuitively, Is the First Contact with Other Dimensional Awareness.**

Though there are many vibrations that make up this world, the basic one is the vibration of the atoms. This vibration can be perceived in the silence (see the technique of listening to the Sound Current), and as one identifies with this vibration, the orientation changes from the body, to the atoms in and around the body. Then one begins to extend the awareness beyond the body, with the realization that he is not leaving the body, but is becoming aware of his larger body, for consciousness is manifest as matter and there is no separation. This realization puts one instantly in tune with all Substance and removes forever the delusive idea that he is alone in this world and separate from Life. This is the spiritual baptism; and along with this experience comes the realization of the finer electricities and finer forces in nature. The inner vision opens and various lights are seen. The light of the atoms vibrating is golden.

22. Meditation on This Atomic Vibration (AUM) Is One Way of Becoming Aware of the Infinite.

There are various techniques given in initiation. One of these is the technique of listening to the Cosmic Sound Current or Atomic Vibration.* Listening to the Sound in meditation gives a focal point for the attention, and the mind of man is led away from the distractions of this world. As one follows (with attention) this sound, the perceptions become keener and keener until the consciousness is lifted through veils of mental activity, lights, feelings and subtle activity, and at last rests in the recognition of pure awareness.

23. Regular Practice of This Technique Leads to Complete Self-realization.

Just as following a river backwards will lead one to its source, so steady attention to the Cosmic Sound will reveal the source, which is unconditioned consciousness.

24. Some Obstacles to Perfect Realization Are Bodily Disability, Mental Laziness, Doubt, Lack of Enthusiasm, Apathy, the Clinging to Experience on This Level, False Perception, Failure to Attain Perfect Concentration, and Failure to Maintain the State of Pure Concentration Once It Is Attained.

---

* This Atomic Vibration is called the Holy Ghost, Sacred Vibration, Aum, Om, The Word.

(A) Bodily Disability

While it is true that there have been some persons who were able to step aside from their bodies and move into the pure awareness, most people will find that the body holds them back if it does not function well. When we are identified with the body, which is loaded with distortions and blockages, physical or mental, it is not a fit instrument for the flow of creative power. Therefore, it is a good idea to keep it in good condition. This may involve physical purification, a change in diet, exercise, and the practice of techniques to purify the nervous system. (All the techniques will aid in this.) Many men are able to ignore the body condition for quite some time, and then in a moment of physical or mental tiredness they find themselves trapped by the body beliefs and negative patterns. It is far better to prevent this by maintaining the body in good order as we unfold in consciousness.

(B) Mental Laziness

It has been found that men and women with keen minds and a high level of awareness make the best students of this science. It is not a matter of learning over the years; it is a matter of becoming aware. Inability, or unwillingness to exercise this faculty is one thing that holds back the progress of many otherwise well conditioned people. It is of great value to learn to think straight and gain control of the mind. Though we come to a point where we transcend the mental activity, it is still a stepping-stone in our practice. The sharper the mind, the more likely it is that the student will make rapid progress.

(C) Doubt

Lack of faith, or lack of the ability to keep the vision of perfection even before it manifests, indicates doubt. It is perfectly normal to doubt that any stage is final, for it is not. But it is important that one never lose the vision of the eternal possibility. Doubt on this matter leads to a negative frame of mind which clouds the perceptions and makes the realization of Pure Consciousness impossible at that stage.

(D) Lack of Enthusiasm

Enthusiasm is required so that the attention may be directed at one point in meditation. Otherwise the mental activity is scattered and there is no attainment. The cure for constant lack of enthusiasm is to keep the company of illumined men and women, either through their writings or in person, or mentally in the silence.

(E) Apathy

This is a state of literal laziness where the world hangs heavy on one's shoulders and the goal seems so far off that it isn't worth the effort. The cure for this is the same as for anyone who lacks enthusiasm.

(F) Clinging to Experience of This Level

When the mind clings to the things of this level of expression, it is impossible to release this contact and extend the awareness. Here we must learn to be detached and see the One Life manifesting *as* creation and break from dependence on things and forms. This does not mean that we have to renounce the world by leaving it, but it does mean that we must come to our real senses.

(G) FALSE PERCEPTION

When a person accepts a part of creation on any level as the ultimate, then he suffers from false perception. A person who believes in this three dimensional world only, is limited. Also, a person who gets a fixation on the psychic plane, mental plane, and even planes of finer perception, is bound to that plane where his vision is anchored. This bondage means stability if that is the plane to express upon; but it is limitation if the inner desire to transcend it comes forth and it cannot be released.

(H) FAILURE TO ATTAIN PERFECT CONCENTRATION

If a person fails in the attempt to attain the perfected vision, this too, is an obstacle. Sometimes the reason for failure is to be found in the fact that attention units are bound up in other areas, as mentioned in earlier paragraphs. At other times we find an actual reluctance to experience a new viewpoint because of its newness, even when we intuitively feel it to be to our advantage.

(I) FAILURE TO MAINTAIN THE STATE OF PURE CONCENTRATION ONCE IT IS ATTAINED

Unless the situations just mentioned are corrected, then in almost every case, even though there is a breakthrough to clear awareness, that perfect vision will not be maintained. Even though it is lost, there will be the aftereffect of power, light, and inspiration as a result of the experience, however fleeting it happened to be. The solution to this problem of slipping from the state of perfect vision is to practice steadily until all the factors are properly adjusted and there is no distraction. We deal with this in the next paragraph.

25. Along with Failure to Maintain the Perfect Concentration, There Is Often the Experience of Pain, Mental Distress, Uncontrolled Movement of the Body, and Misdirected Flow of Life Force.

(A) Pain arises from misunderstanding of the basic principles of life. It is also due to active desire patterns, memories, and emotional shock. Pain is experienced when a person has a compulsive desire and has no way to fulfill it, or when he is always conjuring up desires in order to avoid living happily in the moment. Pain also attends the memory of the painful past. (See method of releasing or revising memories.) Or again, pain can be experienced when a person allows himself to be effect, and reacts unthinkingly to life; but this, too, is the result of incorrect knowledge. When one is anchored in the realization of his true nature, there is no need to have compulsive desire, to be hung up on the past, or react without control to anything that takes place in this world.

(B) MENTAL DISTRESS

Because the experience and understanding is still tied to failure and lack of vision, mental agony is often demonstrated in the life of the student. Such distress often accompanies the emotional memory of guilt, regret and shame.

(C) UNCONTROLLED MOVEMENT OF THE BODY

First, there is the restless activity of the body due to the manifestation of confusion and an attempt to find oneself. This causes a person to run from one point to another, from one source of diversion to another. Then, there is the uncontrolled movement of the body due to the activation of the inner life forces. In deep meditation, when this life force is awakened and pours through the nervous system, due to the fact that there are tensions and energy blockages, the force of the energy flowing causes a tremor of the body. It is not necessary to dramatize, in fact, an effort should be made to relax even more. When complete relaxation is accomplished, the uncontrolled movements will cease. In some cases of deep ecstasy, when there is no desire to remain relaxed, people in the meditation have been known to dance or perform rhythmic movements. This pouring through, of the life force, has a cleansing effect. It is termed the Cosmic Fire and purifies body and mind as it works, and brings about a regeneration of the body.

(D) MISDIRECTED FLOW OF LIFE FORCE

The flow of life force in the body is tied in with the activity of the mind and connected with the action of breathing. When the mind is restless, the life force races about the body and adds to the confusion. To conquer this problem there are techniques of life force control, which greatly aid in the process of self-mastery. Self-mastery is not a matter of forcefully controlling the body and body activities, but is a matter of remaining on the high pinnacle of realization, unmoved by anything which tends to distract the attention.

26. **A Sure Way to Bring the Mental Activity to a Standstill Is to Come to the Point of Detachment.**

To be detached does not mean to flee from this world, but rather to remind oneself of the Power acting in, and as, this world. When this attitude of detachment is complete, the idea of duality fades away; hence all thought of pleasure, pain, happiness and unhappiness is no more.

27. **In Deep Contemplation There Comes the Experience of Breathlessness as All Energies Are Withdrawn from the Body, into the Centers of the Head.**

This is nothing to fear, but is a natural result of deep meditation. Whenever the mind is active, it shows some identification with the body. The restless mind and restless breath prevents the experience of perfect realization. There is no point to holding the breath in an effort to still the mind, although there are techniques for controlling the life force through the instrumentality of the breath action. (See Techniques.)

28. **By Practicing Definite Psycho-physical Exercises It Is Possible to Bring the Body Activities to a Standstill and Experience Acute Awareness.**

One of the most important contributions in this, or any other age, is the group of techniques which make it possible to take a conscious part in self-unfoldment. This is possible through an understanding of how the body and mind works as a unit, *and how it is possible to detach from this body-mind unit at will.* All the philosophy and all the discussion in the world will not take the place of actual experience, which can be had with practice.

29. **As It Is Possible to Come to a Point of Pure Awareness by Bringing the Activities of the Mind and Body to a Standstill, So It Is Possible to Have the Experience by Concentrating on the Light Within.**

A Commentary on Concentration

When we throw the attention within (the center of the forehead and mid-brain) in meditation, and the thoughts settle down, we see the emergence of the white light. This light may take different colors and hues in the beginning, but gradually it will become white. As we focus the attention upon this light, we withdraw from the sense experience and soon we find ourselves in a deep state of concentration. This is a state of intense awareness with perfect control. It has nothing in common with the negative practice of auto-conditioning or subconscious trance, where one loses self-will.

30. This State Can Be Attained by Contemplating on the Knowledge That Comes in Sleep.

It is said that if one will analyze the sleep state, it will be possible to understand all of life. This is because during the sleep process we experience a radical shift of consciousness, which if understood, would open many doors. There are several ways to investigate the sleep process: by watching the transition of consciousness when going to sleep and when awakening; by consciously learning to function in the dream state—that is, be conscious of dreaming and be fully aware of what is going on. (See Techniques.) It is also possible to use the sleep experience as a gateway to other dimensions and as an exit from this body. Also, by comparing the sleeping dream experience with the waking dream (normal consciousness), we come to understand the unreality of this world. With this understanding comes the ability to manipulate the substance of this world at will, just as in the dream state you would not find it hard to believe that you can manipulate the substance of the dream world. This world which appears to be so solid is just as fluid as the dream state seems to be, when we awaken to the truth of the nature of matter.

31. As a Starting Point One Can Meditate upon Any Concept That Seems to Be Close to Reality.

Since it is impossible for many people to perceive the Absolute, it is quite in order to start with the level which can be grasped, with the understanding that any concept is less than the Absolute, but is a point of contact. We see in the beginning many people contemplate a personal deity, or a person who seems to manifest truth. Then the meditation becomes more selective until the necessity of form and personality drops away and the meditation takes on the nature of Spirit to Spirit (Soul to Reality) activity. Because of the various levels of consciousness manifest in men and women, we have the different methods of approaching the Ultimate Reality.

32. One Who Meditates in the Highest Way Finds the Mind Becoming Cleared of Obstructions. The Attention Flows by Degrees, from the Atomic to the Infinite.

As the attention is diverted from this plane, the inner worlds open to the vision. Then there is the contemplation of the atomic vibration, the inner lights and the subtle activities of the vital forces. The strong willed soul, however, never wavers, and moves on until it pierces all veils of illusion and comes to rest in the realization of the Absolute. Just as many people get sidetracked and temporarily lost on this plane, so, many get sidetracked and lost on the astral and mental planes. The way to avoid this is always to have singleness of purpose. There is nothing to fear at any time, for singleness of purpose and implicit faith in the attainment will put everything in its proper place.

33. The Natural Consequence of Proper Meditation Is, the Soul Becomes Cosmic Conscious and Rests in the Realization of Omnipresence.

Good intentions are not enough to insure the cosmic conscious state; but when the mind is emptied of all erroneous conclusions, and the awareness is allowed to extend, it is the natural experience. Successful meditation always results in the experience of oneness. The mind takes on the nature of that which is contemplated; and when it is emptied in deep silence, then it reflects perfection. This is the illumination. A flash of illumination is not enough. One must repeat the experience in order to wipe out all trace of unknowingness and self-consciousness. This is the first experience and is called, in Sanskrit, SabiKalpa Samadhi or that state of realization of the Absolute which is still tinged by some subtle mental activity and wonderment.

34. This First State of Exalted Consciousness Is Temporary, but Is Proof That the Process Is Bearing Fruit.

To have the experience, if only for a short moment, of the Absolute Reality, is to have all doubt wiped away forever. But one must not assume that the goal has been attained at this point. It is a major breakthrough, but because of the activity of the mind on a subtle level, and because the habit of functioning as a self-conscious personality has not been overcome, there is a tendency to slip away from the perfect vision or use the new powers which come from the vision to increase the abilities on this plane. If the motive is proper, this is the desirable thing to do; but if the motives are impure, then such behavior brings increased unhappiness and bondage. *We suffer, not because of the arbitrary will of an omnipresent deity, but because our actions, magnified with new energy, are more productive, so that if the energy is directed into proper channels, the results are spectacular,* but if improperly directed (that is, directed for motives of control or against universal law) then the increased power will naturally result in violent havoc. The more the perception is cleared, the more the necessity for being open for guidance. To receive guidance does not mean that we are going to become dependent upon another person or individual on this or any other plane. It means we are going to open our consciousness to let the Universal Life Current flow through with a minimum of resistance, so that we may be carried along to fulfill our destiny.

35. When the Traces of Mental Activity Fully Subside, Then We Experience Perfect Cosmic Consciousness.

Through practice we gradually dis-identify with subtle mental activities, transcend our desire patterns, lose our need for a body as a point of orientation, and rest in pure awareness. In this state when the mental activity has settled down, we no longer associate with the past; and as there is no concept of past, so there is no idea of the future, but instead the awareness extends to embrace past and future. The realization at this point is Oneness. Past, future, sense of separateness, duality—all are swallowed up in the ever-present beingness. This is not a state of nothingness, but a realization of intense fulfillment. The self-conscious sense is completely annihilated.

36. With Cosmic Consciousness Comes Effortless Realization on All Levels and of All Things.

If the awareness is all-embracing, then there is no longer anything unknown. It may not be that you will know everything consciously, but wherever you direct your attention, you can know. It is not a matter of thinking; it is a matter of knowing. When you want to have the answer to a question or the solution to a problem, you just hold the known factors before the mind's eye and relax. Don't think, just look. And as you do this, the truth will reveal itself to you. This is a pure creative process and is accomplished without dependence upon reference to past experience. With cosmic consciousness comes omniscience or all-knowing. This realization is accompanied by intense bliss and a joy of living.

37. Pure Meditation Leads Ultimately to the Realization of the Absolute or Unmanifest Consciousness.

As long as we see lights, hear sounds, perceive anything separate from our own nature, we have not yet come to the point of perfect realization. When we rest in Beingness, we transcend feelings, even the ecstasy and joy. That is why clinging to the states realized in meditation prevents complete realization, and is the reason for the counsel to renounce even the results of meditation. In order to rise higher in consciousness, we have to release the weights which tend to hold us back, these weights being our concepts, ideas, likes, dislikes and personal desires.

38. Even the Effort to Concentrate Is Evidence of a Sense of Illusion.

While it is true that eventually the practice of meditation itself will fall away when the perfect state of consciousness is experienced, we must not fall into the common error of thinking that meditation is unnecessary. Only when we have completed our work can we feel justified in throwing away our tools. But to discard them with the work only half completed is to invite self-deception. Usually it will be found that the practice of the techniques as put forth in this book will enable you to clear your mind and come to a high state of realization. At this point you can cease the techniques and rest in the state of consciousness that has been reached. The techniques do not produce the state or develop it, but merely clear the confusion from the mind. We are already perfect and whole when we realize who we are, and come to the proper understanding. It is a matter of changing the viewpoint from body and limitation, to consciousness and freedom. When one rests in the realization of the unmanifest state, then he is free from the belief in fluctuating from one level of consciousness to another. He lives. He moves freely through time and space. He does not experience death or a shutting down of awareness, though he may choose to change dimensions and move from body to body. The first stages of Samadhi or Cosmic Perception begin to cancel out other tendencies and desire patterns, and the higher or purer stage causes a complete regeneration and refinement of body and mind on all levels.

BOOK TWO

The Practice of Concentration

THE PRACTICE OF CONCENTRATION

1. **Self-discipline, Study, and Attempting to Rely upon the Infinite Invisible Is the Way to Conscious Union with the Absolute.**

While the mental activity is such that it prevents the realization of Truth, we should practice self-discipline to direct the flow of attention in the right direction. Self-discipline does not mean self-punishment. It simply means to take conscious control of the restless desires and feeling nature and begin to bring some order into the picture.

Then we should study the principles of life, avoiding theory and controversial subjects, which only serve to detract from the real purpose. Healthy investigation which challenges the intellect is good, but overemphasis on the opinions of shallow-minded men simply prolongs the experience of awakening. When we really feel the urge to unfold in consciousness, we find books, teachers, teachings, and situations seeming to come into our life pattern to make it possible to continue the unfoldment. It is at this point, usually, when we are in earnest about the study of life processes, and in our attempt to rely upon the Infinite Invisible for guidance, we are led to make contact with a true Preceptor. In the Oriental teachings the Preceptor is called the Guru or the Awakener. Although the Preceptor may teach, his main function is to awaken us to the realization of our own true nature and inspire us to continue on the path. Without this awakening, we may study for years and round out our fund of knowledge, but still lack the real inner activity which comes as a result of being initiated and awakened. It is more than a change in heart or a new mental concept; it is an actual transformation of consciousness.

Even though the Preceptor usually manifests in a body as a person on this plane, *it is still the impersonal activity of Spirit working through the clear instrumentality of the Preceptor which does the work.* A true Preceptor is an open channel for the flow of Spirit into the lives of those seeking light. A true Preceptor never seeks to use disciples or control them, but only seeks to assist them in their unfoldment. We have only one Preceptor, but many teachers who may assist us in gathering data for intelligent living in society.*

Because of the nature of consciousness and the quality of consciousness which manifests through different individuals, we find a tendency for souls to group together with others of similar nature. This is why sometimes we feel drawn to a certain teaching or line of teachers; and other times, though we recognize a high teaching or a high level of consciousness, we feel no pull toward it because we are not attuned to it. It is not on our wave length. Likewise, we should not expect everyone else to feel drawn to our particular viewpoint and interest in life.

All too often, disciples who mean well will deify their Preceptor and make themselves nothing by comparison. This worship of the form is a hindrance to the unfoldment of consciousness. Recognize in the Preceptor the Light of Spirit flowing to you, but do not personalize it. I do not blame the disciples altogether for this display of extreme

* My Preceptor is Paramhansa Yogananda, and through him I am connected with a vital link of power with Swami Sri Yukteswar, Lahiri Mahasaya and the Master Babaji. While I remain embodied on this or another level and maintain my attunement with this line of Adepts, there is a definite flow of power passing from them through me, and into my work and teaching.

The Practice of Concentration

dependence, for I feel that a true Preceptor, once the contact is made, will make an effort to erase the ignorance and superstition from the mind of the disciple. If he does not, then it would seem to me that there is still much that needs to be corrected in his consciousness.

2. **Our Practice Eventually Leads to the Experience of Perfect Superconsciousness, Which Tends to Minimize the Pain-bearing Obstructions.**

Our practice is not to be taken as an end in itself, but is to lead us to the experience of superconsciousness. Frequent experience of this superconscious state will have the effect of neutralizing the distortion patterns and psychological blockages in the subconscious. The obstructions which cause pain are the distortion patterns which have taken root after being impressed upon the subconscious.

These patterns on a subtle level eventually manifest on the gross level. The time to prevent their manifestation is when they are still on the subtle level and more easily handled. One of the reasons for their being removed in meditation is that the energies in the body rise into the surface nerve channels and this quickening of the vital force erases the patterns.

3. **The Pain-bearing Obstructions Manifest Also: as Ignorance, Egoism, Attachment, Aversion, and Clinging to the Life Form.**

These five erroneous concepts keep man in tune with the shadow world and make it possible for him to remain in confusion. The fastest way to eradicate these concepts is to see that essentially they have no basis in fact except as concepts, and then change the concept. This requires a bit of abstraction, but it can be done. We shall deal with each concept in turn:

A. IGNORANCE. Lack of understanding is ignorance. It has nothing to do with a man's intelligence or social level. If a man lacks understanding in a specific area, then he is ignorant in relationship to it, though he may display brilliance in another area. Brilliance in a specific area does not give a man the right to presume to be Self-realized. It may be true that he is aware of the light of truth in one or more areas, but it is like a searchlight shining in the darkness, making holes of light here and there, but lighting up only a part of the total darkness. Ignorance of his true nature leads man to believe that his senses tell him all there is to know and that he is a body of flesh and lives in the present space-time continuum. This concept is obviously a hindrance to unfoldment.

B. EGOISM. This is the concept that man is separate from the source of life. This concept causes man to feel that he is alone and impotent when he looks at the vastness of the universe and compares it with his own nothingness. A person can pretend to be humble and always shrink from recognition and status but still be egotistical, as long as he accepts the idea of being separate from the rest of the life forms. *Humility is the recognition of this One Life, in, through and as everything.* Humility has nothing to do with bowing and scraping before an imagined deity or towering figure. This is delusion of the worst kind.

C. ATTACHMENT. Attachment to things is an indication that the person does not really understand the truth of the One Life, infinitely manifesting. By being aware of the One Life and by maintaining the realization that everything is presented to you according to your requirement, there is no longer any point in being overly attached to any thing or any person. True, we have our human relationships and our sentimental attachments; and while we are aware of this, we can also be aware of the impersonal nature of Life. Non-attachment does not mean carelessness in regard to the things in this world. *It means a recognition of Consciousness being manifest as the things of this world.* A person in this state of consciousness does not have to retreat from the world, except for periods of meditation and refreshment, for an attempt to escape is an indication of a belief in the power of things and a belief that they have reality apart from the Source.

D. AVERSION. This concept is manifest as extreme dislike or repugnance to anything in this or any world. An extreme objection to anything or any characteristic is an indication that the person with this feeling is believing in a universe divided into segments. While there may be things that you do not care to see in your particular life experience, and levels of consciousness and modes of human conduct that would be bothersome or even objectionable for you, still there should be the realization that anything manifest is an extension of Consciousness and therefore has its place in the scheme of things. This release from feeling aversion is one of the most helpful aids to the realization of cosmic consciousness.

E. CLINGING TO THE LIFE FORM. We will agree that it is helpful to accept the life form, the body, as a necessary contact with this plane. We can accept the fact that the bodies of other people act as contact points for them with this dimension. Yet, we should not allow ourselves to persist in clinging to the belief in the form as being necessary for eternal expression. Neither should we feel a sense of loss when the form fades from sight, if the mission of the soul has been accomplished.

We should shift our attention from the concept that Spirit is confined to form and recognize that It is free to operate with or without a form, as It desires. Clinging to one's own body form when it is obvious that the need for it has passed, leads to the pathetic sight of catering to the body in a futile effort to preserve it. Clinging to the form of another leads to grief when that form passes from view, and often leads one into months and years of fruitless search for the personality through contact with mediums or in the silence of one's own meditation.

It is true that we all meet souls with whom we share mutual feelings and aspirations. The fact that one soul or another changes dimensions need not mean a separation of consciousness from the dimension. In the part of the book on Techniques you will learn how to tune in with a soul on any level and bring him before your inner vision.*

10. The Fine Subtle Impressions Are to Be Resolved into Their Causal State.

As the above-mentioned concepts are created from the realm of mind and formed from subtle impressions, the easiest manner of overcoming them is to resolve them back to their causal state and wipe them out. Working from the outside in is a long way around. Many people spend years trying to understand the mind and personality in order that they might have peace. Others spend their time and substance endeavoring to transform their per-

---

* The above commentary explains the material contained in verses 3-9.

The Practice of Concentration

sonality, not realizing that the fastest and surest way, both to understand and transform the mind and personality, is to attune to the level of subtle patterns which is the cause of the mind and personality conditionings and work from that level. In deep meditation we actually come to the level of awareness where we see the subtle mental impressions that are the cause of the mental attitude and personality as revealed by surface indications.

11. In Deep, Silent Meditation the Gross Modifications of the Subtle Impressions Are Understood and Released.

The goal of meditation and the mystical experience is to attain conscious awareness of the Ultimate Reality. While this is unfolding, there are many important side effects, one being the release of the subtle impressions that are the cause of concepts which lead to ignorance and pain.

This takes place on many levels. For instance, with the experience of illumination comes instantaneous revelation and release from limitation. The renewing of the mind due to the experience of illumination transforms the entire character and conduct of the person who has the experience. This is due to the infiltration of the Light and Power into the body, mind and eventually the affairs of the person. There is the experience of a tremendous quickening of the dormant life force, which is awakened and directed through the body on all levels. This has a cleansing effect as it sweeps aside many subtle patterns and brings an awakening of vitality to body parts heretofore sleeping. There is a natural tendency for the pure consciousness and the gross, manifest (body) consciousness to meet at the highest possible level, *and this results* in a tremendous refinement of body and mental power. As the urge of the soul to express pushes forward, new areas of consciousness are opened in the body, upper spine and brain centers. This action over a period of time will create a superior type of organism through which the soul may express with little or no hindrance.

12. **The Sum Total of Reactive Patterns Are Contained in the Desire Body and Are Manifest Now or at Some Other Point in Time and Space.**

Just so long as the reactive patterns exist, we can be sure of seeing their manifestations in the present or in the future. All desires must be fulfilled and thus voided, or they can be voided by the practice of techniques of meditation. Or, they can be modified by intelligent work in the silence. Desires or psychological blocks which cause us to be pulled to and fro in this world must be erased if we are to be free.

13-14. **The Patterns Existing on the Subtle Level Give Rise to Experiences of Pleasure and Pain, and Manifestation in Bodies of Various Types.**

The patterns of desire and reaction, working out their balance, cause man to experience pleasure and pain to the extent that they bring about experiences that fit into his conscious life scheme, or not, and they also determine the type of body the soul will inhabit in the future, either by causing a modification of the present body or by the creation of a body when the soul incarnates again. The experiences now viewed are tied in with the existing subtle patterns and the body now viewed is a perfect form

The Practice of Concentration

according to the subtle pattern. These reactive patterns are of three types. They are:

1. *Latent Patterns.* The deep-seated patterns that have been received as psychic impressions, but which have been received unconsciously or have been consciously forgotten. These patterns rest in an inactive state awaiting some situation to trigger them off, then they come to the surface.

2. *Active Patterns.* Those patterns which are now in the process of manifesting.

3. *New Reactive Patterns.* These are the patterns being *set* in the desire body due to present reaction to life and presently acquired desires. The way to handle these patterns in order is to be aware of existing patterns that cause you to act and feel as you do. When you are aware of them, you can either modify them or let them work out, according to your decision. Then through meditation you can become intuitively aware of the latent desire patterns and either modify them or erase them as you feel led to do. *The way to avoid creating new patterns which will control you in the future is to come to the level of consciousness where you act spontaneously and in harmony with the laws of life.* When you do this, you are not hurt; therefore you do not accept reactive patterns, and you do not entertain compulsive desire. As a result, you do not find yourself helplessly pushed into undesirable experiences.

15. **To the Man in the State of Illumination, Any Experience in a Body of Any Kind Is Considered Pain in Relationship to the Freedom of Illumination. This Is Because Identification with the Qualities of Consciousness Bring About Consequences, Anxiety and Subconscious Impressions.**

While it is true that in the right state of consciousness the soul can operate a body and be fully aware of what is going on, from the viewpoint of the disembodied soul, any ensnarement in a body of any kind—causal, astral or physical—is a painful experience because it dims the consciousness in small measure. An illumined soul must agree to delusion just a little bit in order to manifest a body.

And, with the identification of the body and the world in which the body lives, there is an attunement with the laws of that level, thus an entanglement with circumstances. There is also anxiety because of anticipation of loss or fulfillment. In this situation there is slight identification with the pleasure-pain motivation and thus a tendency to crave more experiences which will bring happiness, and avoid the experiences which bring pain or frustration. Also, being in tune with other life forms, there is the tendency to accept the flow of impressions and let them mingle in the subconscious, giving rise to more confusion.

16. The Pain Which Will Come as a Result of the Manifestation of Negative Patterns Can Be Avoided.

This is one of the most often quoted statements in connection with this science of mystical union. By eradicating the latent patterns, which if allowed to manifest, would cause pain, then the pain can be avoided. This viewpoint is not for the timid-minded who feel they must suffer for past mistakes, real or imagined, but it is for those energetic souls who desire to cut through the shambles of confusion and rise in Light and Power. *The truth that man need not suffer for the mistakes of the past is one of the most welcome, yet incomprehensible, principles of life.*

Many of the negative patterns existing on the subconscious level, which will one day manifest if not neutralized, are not the result of personal mistakes, but simply the result of impressions being given to the subconscious mind, either by another during an emotional scene, or while the one receiving the impression was unconscious of the impression being directed, or simply as the result of a race idea or human concept being accepted without being challenged.

17. The Concept of Illusion Which Arises When the Soul Identifies with the Reactive Level of the Mind Is the Cause of the Pain Which Is to Come.

This is the basic principle, which if understood, will free man from every form of bondage. The soul mistakenly assumes itself to be the body; and as the body, with the mind and the reactive patterns, it is subject to the laws of the body at this particular point in time and space.

18. The Object of Perception (the Body) Is Composed of Elements and Organs—the Qualities of Consciousness Which Make Possible the Experiences in Life. The Understanding of the Body Nature and the Qualities of Consciousness Makes It Possible for the Soul to Attain Liberation.

Here we have in concise form, the nature of the created world, its reason for being and the possibility of understanding it. The body is created from the universal substance and adheres to a definite pattern. In order for consciousness to manifest and experience motion, there must be qualities of consciousness. These qualities are three: the elevating quality, the activating quality and the quality of inertia. These three qualities can be seen in every manifestation of nature and make it possible for consciousness to act upon itself. This gives the appearance of division of consciousness.

19. **The Three Qualities of Consciousness Have Four Divisions: The Specific Manifestation, the Nonspecific, the Indicated and the Invisible.**

Here we see a bit deeper into the nature of the manifestation of forms visible to the eye. We see material form about us and we know that consciousness is manifesting. Then we have the non-specific or the divisions not readily obvious to the ordinary sight, and they are: the senses, the subtle energies, and the vital life forces. The fact that we are aware of the manifesting form and the existence of life forces indicates the existence of basic material substance, or atomic matter, and the required subdivisions of that. And, since common sense (plus intuitive insight) tells us that all this cannot exist by itself, we predicate the existence of pure consciousness, out of which everything has been extended and upon which everything else depends. The invisible is more real than any of its divisions, yet least known to the majority of people in this present age.

20. **The Soul, or That Which Perceives, Is Pure Knowledge, but in Observing Ideas It Does So Through the Medium of Mind, Which Is Conditioned by Surrounding Impressions.**

In the purest sense, the soul is knowledge itself, being one with pure consciousness. But as it desires to perceive,

The Practice of Concentration

it must postulate the existence of something separate from itself, and then must view this separate existence through the filter of the mind. The mind being an individualization of universal mind is prone to receive impressions from without and will be conditioned ever so slightly by the acceptance of the impressions. Therefore when the soul uses the mind to perceive, that which is perceived is not correctly perceived but is distorted according to the modification of the mind. If a person wears colored glasses, then everything viewed through them will be tinged with the color of the glass.

21-22. Everything That Exists Is for the Sake of the Soul That Perceived It, and When the Soul Attains Self-realization, the Objective World Will Cease to Be for Him.

Because the soul can perceive the world about it, this world for the time being is its field of operation. It is for the purpose of experience and activity. When through the practice of the principles as put forth in this book, man is able to bring the mental activity to a standstill, he ceases to view this objective creation. *The stilling of the mental activity and the blanking out of conscious awareness are two different things.* The former is practiced and brings an increasing awareness and a transcendence of creation, but the blanking out of awareness is an avoidance technique and leads to greater darkness and bondage. There is a difference between *becoming everything* and on the other hand *becoming nothing*. This chapter contains the precise methods to use to expand the conscious awareness, and the last section of the book, containing the techniques to be used in meditation, will make it possible for you to practice intelligently.

23-24. Ignorance Causes the Soul to Identify with the Mind and That Which Is Perceived by the Mind.

This has been the subject of the last few paragraphs and will not be further elaborated upon at this point.

25-26. When Ignorance Is Wiped Out, There Is the Breaking of the False Identification and Thus Automatic Liberation of Soul Is Assured.

Ignorance is removed by resolving it to the idea state and then by seeing the nothingness of it.

27. The Progression of Unfoldment Is Measured in Seven Stages.

Man, being firmly identified with the body and material world, begins to awaken and continues to do so progressively through seven stages, though there are degrees of awakening within each stage. There is no real virtue in comparing two or more souls at a certain stage, for though their experience will be similar, the quality will differ. These stages in order of progression are:

A. Material consciousness, or consciousness of this world. With this awareness is the belief in the reality of material objects and the conformity to the laws of action and reaction. There is also the acceptance of mass believing.

B. This level of consciousness is apparent when man begins to be aware, on a subtle level, of the fine electricities within matter. Here he begins to practice the techniques of life force control and learns to consciously

The Practice of Concentration

direct the flow of the life forces in the body. He also becomes aware of the activity of life forces about him. This usually leads him to make contact with a Preceptor, who helps him awaken the perceptions of feeling and which experience leads him to the next stage.

C. At this point, since ignorance is being overcome, the inner world is being revealed. This is the astral level, and when one is aware at this point, he is clairvoyant and sees into astral planes according to his desire and sensitivity. He sees auras about physical bodies. He is aware of his own astral body or body of light and is able to see it by looking within the third eye where the body will be reflected. A person on this level will move effortlessly into the astral world when the time comes for leaving the body.

D. *The next stage is the intermediate point where creation really steps down and manifestation takes place.* This is the point where the ideas in universal mind begin to be reflected in the world, starting on the energy level. Every person must move in consciousness through this level, and this level is called the door to the kingdom of Spirit. No one can avoid it in the unfolding experience.

E. This fifth stage is the level of thought forms and here the idea of separate existence takes place. It is beyond the level of form or creation and anyone with the belief in bodies finds this level incomprehensible, except as a concept. The body worn by the soul as it passes into this phase is of the most luminous nature, and as the realization of this level becomes more pronounced, the body gradually disappears.

F. The sixth stage is unknown to any except those who have dropped the identification with form and ideas. It is the level of universal harmony and balance. Here the soul experiences bliss and serenity.

G. The final stage is Reality. *That which Is. The Absolute, beyond vibration, light or feeling.*

The Eight Steps to Mystical Union

28. The Practice of the Science Which Leads to the Mystical Union Is Made Possible by the Purification of the Various Bodies and the Eradication of Ignorance.

As a result of steady practice in the right direction, the sincere student experiences progressive stages of enlightenment which culminates in illumination of consciousness. The practice of techniques, purification, discrimination and discernment leads to perfection. There must be balance in the practice and a real desire to experience the ultimate fulfillment. This is really a two-way process, as we must take the time and make the effort in the right direction until we get the initial contact; then it becomes easier as we are pulled to the Center by an attractive force. The conscious attempt to purify the body through right diet, proper exercise and good habits makes it easier to purify the feeling nature by raising the quality of desire and experience. This, along with a conscious attempt to eradicate the negative mental attitudes, will prepare the way for the experience of meditation. We shall deal with these stages in the next few pages, as we get into the most practical part of this instruction.

29. The Eight Steps to Successful Practice Are: The Five Restraints, the Five Observances, Correct Meditation Posture, Control of Life Force, the Interiorization of the Mental Activity, Concentration, Meditation, and Ultimate Union.

The Practice of Concentration

These eight steps should be clearly understood, for they hold the key to rapid unfoldment. We will discuss them in detail.

30-31. The Five Restraints Are: Harmlessness, Truthfulness, Non-stealing, Continence, and Non-receiving. These Rules Remain Consistent Regardless of Time, Point in Space, Opinions or Need for Expediency, for They Are Universal Principles.

(1) HARMLESSNESS. We will find as we cover these various points that they can be related to all levels of human behavior. Harmlessness is established when the desire to hurt another is removed, not merely suppressed. This is not the same as the attitude of "I won't hurt you if you won't hurt me." Neither does it spring from fear of reaction to an attempt on our part to harm another. It arises from the realization that since we are part of the whole, it is incongruous to even assume that there is a separate person or thing to be acted upon. When this attitude is established, *we find that others do not desire to harm us*. The great furor raised over the preservation of the life form often springs from ignorance of man's eternal nature and is not the same as the recognition of the Totality of being.

(2) TRUTHFULNESS. Truthfulness is established when one is consistent with universal principle in every action. To attempt to be untruthful is an attempt to hide a portion of consciousness from itself, and this of course cannot be done. What happens in the attempt is that the mind suppresses certain facts and remains self-deceived. A mind filled with distortions cannot experience enlightenment. When a person lives in Truth Consciousness, he has the power to directly manifest his spoken word. Since

all distortion is gone from the mind, whatever is desired and willed into expression is carried through into manifestation. At this level of realization comes the understanding of universal supply, for nothing is hidden; therefore, anything can be revealed, as the attention is turned to it. A true Adept is freed from the idea of working for supply, which would be an indication of a belief in action and reaction and contrary to the realization of Truth Consciousness. *At this point of consciousness, the Adept simply stretches forth his hand with the knowledge that even before he grasps the object of his desire, it will be in the process of manifestation and will materialize through normal channels to meet him at the moment of acceptance.*

(3) NON-STEALING. Stealing on this level is when a person tries to appropriate what belongs to another by right of consciousness, sometimes through force, sometimes through stealth. Since our environment is the reflection of our believing, and that which is ours according to the mental equivalent will come into our life pattern to the degree that we can accept it, without force or coercion of any kind, *we have but to stand and see the fulfillment of the law.* When we are in harmony with the law, there are no exceptions to the rule. When we come to the point in consciousness where we recognize the fullness of consciousness being what is, we can manifest wealth (to the eyes of the world), as we know the truth about universal substance taking form to meet our level of belief.

(4) CONTINENCE. Energy is maintained and properly directed by the practice of continence. Continence means the restraint and proper direction of the energy at our disposal. This relates to every level of activity. Due to partial understanding or an overconcern with the genera-

tive function, many books stress this rule in relation to the sexual experience only. And because people have long identified this function with man's lower nature, many potential illuminates have experienced prolonged periods of ignorance due to their attempt to suppress this urge on the physical level. Suppression of any urge leads to emotional unbalance. The secret of continence is controlled attention, for life force follows the direction of attention.

Intelligent direction of the life forces in the body brings happiness to the organism and gives control to the person who practices. It does not hold true that spiritual experience is the result of suppressing desire. This is covered in more detail in our discussion on asceticism, but let me make it clear at this point that a wholesome understanding of the movement of life force through the body on all levels is the goal of life on this plane. It is not the moving of life force through the sense channels that causes spiritual deadness, *it is the compulsive urge to seek the fulfillment of desire through the sense experience only, that causes trouble*. The urge to experience pleasure through sensual perception is really a perversion of the urge of the soul to realize itself.

In fact, there is a school of thought which instructs the student to live fully in this world with the realization that the life forces are the activities of Spirit, thus there is realization in the human experience, rather than a shutting down of awareness. Most of the trouble in this area springs not from the act of using the sense channels, but from the sense of guilt by association, which is in turn caused by ignorance. What we are concerned with in this particular discussion is the wasting of the vitality that could better be used to strengthen the body and reinforce the subtle energies in the nerve centers. The depletion of vital forces, of course, makes it difficult for the sincere student to be effective in ordinary activities. It would be better for most people to experience life on this level, in line with common sense, rather than be constantly disturbed by unfulfilled desire.

(5) NON-RECEIVING. This is a subtle suggestion. It implies that a person should recognize that anything that comes into his life comes as a direct result of the mental equivalent being established. Thus, man never receives; he merely accepts what life has to offer. Receiving in the relative sense is tied in with the counsel on honesty. The reason that we should recognize that anything given is the result of our acceptance level being established and is the door through which it enters our life experience, is because if we go along with the idea that a person can give us anything, then we personalize the act and tend to feel obligated. While it is the proper thing to be appreciative of the channel through which life flows to meet our desire, we must not in any way, feel bound by the act, any more than we should obligate others by the giving of gifts. To expect to own that which is not ours by right of consciousness and to control others by the giving of favors is to deal on the reactive level of consciousness, and this is full of pitfalls.

About the time that a person truly comes to the point where he understands this truth, he is standing on such a plateau of revelation that he lives in the present with full spiritual awareness. *Pictures of past lives, which are nothing more than memories and have no real value, often comes to the surface of the mind.* The reactive patterns, positive and negative, associated with these memories, are released when this happens. Then we have the experience of great loads of pain and emotional turmoil being released.

If you find that your practice of the techniques in meditation is not bringing the expected results, then review this section of the book to be sure that you are really paving the way for enlightenment by getting clear on these subtle points. Without understanding the significance of these points, you will only experience a partial awakening.

32. **The Five Main Observances Are: Internal and External Purification, Contentment, Mental Discipline, Study and the Recognition of the Infinite Invisible at All Times.**

We have discussed the five restraints and their purpose. Now we shall deal with the five observances in order. But before we do, let us remind ourselves of the obstructions to the attainment of the mystical union and the method of avoiding them.

33. **To Control Thoughts Which Are Contrary to Proper Practice, One Should Make a Definite Attempt to Control the Mental Attitude.**

This includes the conscious attempt to replace negative thoughts with constructive thoughts, and this is greatly facilitated by our being properly motivated. The reading of inspirational materials and the company of inspired men and women will help us to experience right motivation.

34. The Obstructions to the Accomplishment of the Mystical Union Are Those Mentioned in This Part of the Book (See Above) Whether Committed, Caused, or Approved; Either Through Mental Selfishness, Anger or Ignorance; Whether Slight, Medium or Powerful in Intensity; and Result in Greater Ignorance and Unhappiness. This Should Also Be a Motivation to Control the Intentions and Desires.

To live in complete or even partial agreement with the mortal tendencies is to experience a sense of separateness from Spirit, to the degree of the identification. Every agreement to the truth of the negative characteristics is a thought directly contrary to the realization of truth consciousness. There is no exception to the rule. A contrary thought will produce its manifestation, for this too is the law of mind in action. The manifestation is in direct ratio to the degree of agreement with the thought.
* (See footnote.)

40. The Result of Internal and External Purification Is That the Soul Recognizes the Body Form as Distinct from Itself.

Purification is, of course, deeper than physical. While the conscientious student will take good care of the body, keeping it well fed and healthy, he will also make an attempt to purify the mental and emotional nature by adhering to the rules of proper conduct as outlined here. The result of such physical, mental and emotional puri-

---

* Verses 35-39 are passed over here, as the material is included in the commentary under verses 30-31.

The Practice of Concentration

fication is that through the experience of partial enlightenment, there comes a realization of the true nature of soul and body and their relationship. In the beginning stages the soul does not like to mingle with other bodies because of the conflict in viewpoint and vibration.

41. As a Result of Purification of the Elevating Quality of Consciousness, There Arises Serenity of Mind, Ability to Concentrate, Conscious Control over the Organs of the Body and a Preparedness for the Full Impact of Illumination.

Internal purification carried to its logical conclusion dissolves the deadening and activating qualities of consciousness, leaving only the elevating quality. From purification of this quality comes the ability to perceive truth directly. There arises a serenity of the mental aspect because of the infiltration of pure consciousness. As this takes place and the mental debris is washed out through the action of this Light, there comes the natural ability to focus the attention at will and concentrate without distraction.

Through the power of concentration in meditation comes the ability to consciously direct the life forces in the body, and the control of the life forces gives control over the organs of the body, as they are dependent upon the flow of life force to maintain their function. The ability to control the organs and bring them to a high level of efficiency prepares the body to receive the liberating shock of cosmic consciousness. While it is true that some people have received illumination while using a broken body, it is a more impressive experience when it manifests through a sound body.

Surface efforts to bring about bodily well-being are

usually fruitless but awareness of the body, even to the level of the atomic structure, which comes in deep meditation, makes it possible to prepare the body for the inflow of power. The average person's body is not prepared for the tremendous flow of life force that accompanies even the initial stages of enlightenment, hence the necessity of practicing some form of meditation to condition the body and refine the nervous system.

42. From Contentment Comes Superlative Happiness.

Contentment is the result of freedom from impressions that cause unwanted experiences. This is best attained when the mind is detached from objects and there is a partial recognition of the true state of things. With understanding there comes a natural contentment and this, deepened in meditation and mingled with serenity becomes bliss. This is not to be confused with the temporary euphoria which attends an emotional release. This is a state which appears as reactive patterns are displaced and the soul nature emerges.

43. Through Mental Discipline Comes Perfection of the Body and Control over the Organs and Senses.

By directing the flow of attention and by getting the mental apparatus under complete control, the body comes under the conscious control of the practicing student. Control over the organs is the result of life force control and awareness of the body on all levels. Man cannot control that of which he is not aware. Man cannot control the body or his environment if he is not aware of the body and the larger body, or environment. From control over the body comes control over the environment, not by

The Practice of Concentration

some magical process, but due to the simple fact that the body is a miniature universe, and understanding of the body nature gives insight into the nature of the universe.

We will soon get to the processes of life force control which gives realization of, and control over, the organs of the body.

44. The Understanding of Word Symbols Brings Realization of the Pattern Behind Them.

This verse relates to the use of words in various situations. First of all, the sincere student is urged to study in order to seek out truth. Now, many students study everything they can get their hands on and their exhaustive research only leads them deeper into the mire of confusion, until eventually they give up in disgust. This is because they have not yet learned to catch the meaning behind the symbol, and instead, have been filing symbols away in the subconscious mind. They confuse the acquisition of data with understanding and miss the point entirely. It even gets worse if they become proud of their skill in handling words without understanding the import of the words.

The secret of proper study is to endeavor to discern the truth behind the symbol. When you get the knack of seeing the truth in scripture, you then find it a simple thing to open the door to the wonderland hidden to less perceptive minds. Through practice you will learn to sift truth from theory and fact from opinion. Study is helpful as it inspires us to come to the realization of our true nature. Study which leads into a maze of endless mental quandary is a diversion from the purpose of true study.

While words are necessary on this level, they fail to convey the full impact of truth. However, the writings of self-realized souls carry a peculiar force due to the conviction of the writer, and this is felt when we read such material. For this reason it is better to read material either by, or about highly realized souls. The vibration that such a work carries will tend to bring us to a similar level of consciousness.

In using prayer or affirmation of any kind, always try to get behind the words to the significance of the words, and then you will find results forthcoming. This is the scientific method of using prayer and affirmation. Prayer to another personality or to a projected idea of deity is unheard of in the practice of advanced souls. There is nothing to pray to, for you, yourself, contain everything when you expand your consciousness and realize it.

A true student never uses words or prayers to make things happen or to control the forces of nature without inner direction. Such methods are for the sorcerers and occultists who are identified with the lower qualities of consciousness. The secret is to get behind the symbol and come to the realization of truth; then everything is revealed.

45. By Releasing All Desires and by Contemplating the Great Light, Comes Union with the Light.

By releasing the desire for any manifestation and by contemplating the Light of pure consciousness, comes union with that Light. This is termed *samadhi* in the Sanskrit language, and is most descriptive. This is the result of the law fulfilling itself. *The soul becomes what it contemplates; therefore when it can release its hold on things and contemplate its own true nature, it experiences fulfillment.* This Light which is contemplated is not an astral light, but the Light of pure consciousness. While it is true that in a sense, the unmanifest consciousness has no light, the stage perceived in illumination is the stage of Light.

This Light can be experienced to such an extent that all awareness of the body is eclipsed. This is the initial stage of samadhi or mystical union, but because of mental impressions on the subtle level that have not yet been eradicated, the soul again identifies with the mind and body. Through steady practice of resting in this Light, the subtle impressions are gradually erased until the experience of Light is stabilized, even when the consciousness is centered in the body. Then it seems as though the body is an extension of the soul consciousness, which indeed it is, and then we have the continuous experience of the perfect superconscious state. At this point we become the *living free* as we move from inner impulse in harmony with natural law.

46. The Proper Meditation Posture Is That Which Is Firm and Pleasant.

Now we come to the actual practice of meditation. First of all, we concern ourselves with the proper posture; one that will afford us a comfortable position so that we can forget the body while we are engaged in meditation. The best posture is upright in the seated position. Many people feel inclined to think that they can meditate while lying down, but this usually brings conflict because this posture is the usual one for sleeping and by subconscious association we often find a tendency to actually go to sleep if we try to meditate in this position. Of course in the case of real injury to the back that has not been corrected, we can make allowances.

It will be better to have a place to meditate where the

atmosphere is pleasant and quiet. This will be uplifting and helpful in setting up the proper mental attitude. A chair that will give the body adequate support and yet allow the spine to be upright and away from the back of the chair will be the best. It is best to avoid any undue pressure on the body, so that we will not be hindered by association with the body.

Students in the Orient, or those with a predisposition for sitting cross-legged, may find this more comfortable than sitting in a chair. In any case, the important thing is to find a sitting position which is comfortable and suitable for a prolonged period of meditation.

47. **By Lessening the Natural Tendency for Restlessness and by Meditating on the Infinite, the Meditation Posture Becomes Firm and Pleasant.**

We lessen the natural tendency for restlessness as we find a suitable place for meditation and prepare to relax. We also find as we meditate on the nature of the Infinite, the attention is taken from the body, and shortly the posture automatically becomes steady and comfortable. Remember the importance of meditating on the Infinite. Many students in the beginning, meditate on the body and the more they do this, the more tense they become. *From form to formlessness through meditation is the goal.*

48. **Correct Posture Being Accomplished, the Dualities Do Not Obstruct Meditation.**

Since most of our concepts of duality are connected with our association with the body, it is obvious that if we can master the proper meditation posture and really change the viewpoint from form to formlessness (from

The Practice of Concentration

body to the Infinite), we can be free of the idea of duality, which is an obstruction to the process of meditation.

49. When the Proper Meditation Posture Is Established, Then the Control of the Movement of the Life Forces in the Body Comes as the Next Step.

Here is one of the most misunderstood parts of the whole book. We are now concerned with the regulation and understanding of the flow of the vital forces in the body. This is not to be confused with breathing exercises, where by rhythmic breathing and suspension of breathing we try to control the forces of the body. It is true that because the life force flowing through the body causes, among other things, the action of inspiration and expiration, and that because this is a convenient place to make contact with, and control the life force, our primary concern is not the regulation of the breath, but the control of the vital forces.

The term used in Sanskrit is *prana* and this signifies the cosmic energy around us and, of course, within us. As all forms are suspended in this ocean of energy and dependent upon it, it stands to reason that an understanding of it, and the ability to control it, gives control over the forces of nature. That this is literally true is evidenced in the lives of the successful exponents of this science.

According to the free flow of this vital energy through the centers of the body, or the lack of free flow, will the body manifest radiant health or dullness and fatigue. The free flow of this energy is a requirement for perfect function of the body.

The understanding of the movement of the life force and its function at various levels of activity, brings a harmony in relationship to the various bodies that are interpenetrated, and which serve as vehicles for the soul on the physical, astral, etheric and mental levels simultaneously.

50. The Modifications of the Life Force in the Body Are Either External, Internal, Motionless and Regulated by Time and Number, and Either Long and Short in Movement.

I am glad to put an end to the fears and ideas of danger, usually attributed to the control of the vital forces, by well-meaning but unrealized teachers and writers. It is easy to label anything as dangerous if little or nothing is known about it. It is also a sign of fear and lack of realization.

Through the use of rhythmic breathing exercises, it is possible to vitalize the body and even perform some rather startling feats as a result of blending the subtle forces with the physical organism. This enables a practitioner of life force control to master his body and the bodies of others. This is a rather low level of operation and is used by the primitive types of man whose nature is still attuned with the deadening and activating qualities of consciousness. Many medicine men and wonder workers are skilled on this level of life force control, but it should be avoided by the person who desires to find release so that he might operate from the highest level.

The internal modification of life force is brought about by an intelligent understanding of the vital centers in the body and of the pouring of the energies through these centers. As a result of deep practice and an awakening of the feeling nature, there comes a realization of the cosmic power that lies sleeping at the center of every material

The Practice of Concentration

form, even in the body of man. This dormant power* is the power which rests at the heart of the atom after the creation of the atom. When it is intuitively perceived, a portion of it begins to activate and moves through the body, through the vital centers and eventually through the entire body, until the body is brought to a high level of vibration and is cleansed by this mighty cosmic fire. The proper use of the techniques to be found in the fifth section of this book, along with the understanding of the laws of behavior stressed earlier, will make it possible to understand the action and experience the full import of this great power.

When one has this power awakened within, then it is possible to stimulate the motion of it in the body of another who is receptive. *This takes place during initiation and is accomplished as the one performing the initiation confronts the Initiate and, by laying on the hands or by merely invading the energy field, extends his realization and brings about a quickening of the vital force of the one seeking awakening.* Following this, is the instruction in meditation and in the technique of consciously directing the flow of life force.

The motionless modification of the life force is accomplished in meditation when the action is brought to a standstill and there is no dramatization of subconscious reactive patterns. This motionless state is effected when the life currents in the body are brought into the central spinal cord and there results a suspension of internal activity. This enables a person to withdraw the attention at will from the objective world, thus cutting him off from the cause of impressions and distraction. A person with this control, who can withdraw the life force from the senses, from the organs of the body, and into the spine

* Termed Kundalini in Sanskrit.

and brain, can at will interiorize the attention and experience union with the Light of Superconsciousness.

The regulation of time and number in relationship to the life forces is tied in with the manifestation of consciousness in form through various levels, resulting in vibration, colors of light and degrees of density of universal substance. The laws of periodicity also apply in connection with the manifestation, for creation is in eternal motion, and the outpicturing of the ideas of universal mind and the indrawing of the creation is a never-ending process. This is a great mystery to the limited mind which tries in vain to find a beginning to the process of creation. The beginning at a particular point in space is when the outward motion begins from the Center, and the end is when it returns to a state of rest for as long as it was extended, before it again moves outward. *Space is established, then particles attach to points of dimension, then the play begins and the grand deception is woven to the mind of man.* But to one who sits in the realization of this cosmic drama, the most amazing thing is the simplicity of it.

The length of the movement of life forces determines the degree of activity in the body of man and his interrelationship with the cosmic dream creation of which he is an integral part. The currents of Life force slice through his body at the centers of vital activity and as a body-oriented soul, he is part and parcel of this magnificent cosmic activity.

51. There is a Fourth Modification of This Life Force and It Transcends the Previously Mentioned Ones.

By steady practice, the life force is perfectly balanced and brings about an alignment of the various bodies and

The Practice of Concentration

also an alignment with the cosmic forces, which are, in turn, modifications of the one universal power. As we come to the realization of the Power, we learn to operate from that level and see the automatic movement of energies, force fields and lines of magnetism as a result of our decision on that high level. Since our vision at all times remains clear, we can see what is taking place; and since we are detached from the manifestation, we do not become entangled and suffer from confusion. People who work with energies, force fields, energy flows, thought control and the like, eventually wind up enslaved in the manifest world because they lose their way in the process. Hence the advice that I give, to work from the level of recognition, rather than get involved with the practice of magnetic healing and mental magic, which includes the use of hypnotism. The hypnotic route is not the route to self-knowledge. Only wishful thinking and a compulsion to "try anything" leads to this conviction. The use of hypnosis is an indication that the operator lacks pure perception as to the nature of consciousness, but of course it is sensible as a method of getting into the subconscious to remove blockages and give immediate relief when no other method is known. It is a tool to be used by the mental therapists but is not needed by a true Adept. Hypnosis depresses certain brain centers and inhibits free will. It leaves a permanent psychic scar if repeated on the subject over a period of time. This psychic scar or impression acts as a lock and holds the consciousness in a depressed condition in that area until it is released. Instead of bringing illumination, it suppresses the activity of consciousness. Persons who submit to repeated sessions of hypnotic trance are making it that much more difficult in the long run, and they soon lose their self-determinism. They may feel energetic and purposeful for a time, but it is due to a compulsive conditioning instead of the urging of the soul endeavoring to express.

52. Through Conscious Recognition of Truth, the Mental Impressions Covering the Light of Pure Consciousness Are Removed.

By understanding the activity of the cosmic life force in the body and in nature, and by holding to the recognition of Truth Consciousness, the desire patterns and subtle mental impressions which give the soul the illusion of being separated from pure consciousness are removed. This brings about a refining of the bodies and eventually the light of the soul shines through in full power.

53. When This Is Attained, the Mind Becomes Fit for Perfect Concentration.

It is possible to be aware of the soul nature and yet have the sense of being individualized. Now is the time for the soul to contemplate the pure consciousness and identify with it. This is possible now that all distractions have been removed, and the light can be steadily perceived within. This leads to abstraction or the interiorization of the mind.

54. The Interiorized Mind Is the Result of the Mind Giving Up the Identification with the Objects Formerly Perceived.

Through the practice of sitting in the silence and by becoming aware of life on all levels, and by focusing the attention in the center of the head, at the point between the eyebrows, the life force in the body is withdrawn from the external organs and senses. This results in the attention being switched off from the objects formerly perceived, or the things of this world. Being disconnected from the things of this world, it is easy to experience the interiorization of the mental faculties as the attention is directed back to the source, and the mind rests in the inner Light of the Soul nature. It is at this point that one can be aware of the mental activities of other people and intuit the desire patterns of the body or the planet. *However, since this is the fifth step in the unfolding experience, it is wise to keep the attention properly directed and avoid the diversion of exploring inner space, exciting as it may seem.*

As the attention is withdrawn and the mind contemplates the light within, it ceases to project new ideas and thus the mind is transcended. That which many have tried to accomplish through years of intellectual effort, through agonizing hours of debate and mental acrobatics, has at last been experienced. This is not an unconscious state or mental blocking; it is an intense realization of the vastness of the unconditioned mind. The mind now becomes an instrument, consciously directed, and the filter through you may view this dimension. It is yours to use as you see fit, as you work from the new level of understanding.

55. From Mastery of This State Comes Supreme Control of the Organs.

This means not only control of the organs of the body, but the organs used by the soul; the bodies on every level, and the complex mental apparatus which is attached to them. From the viewpoint of soul consciousness, you view the mind, the body on all levels, and you know they are objects of perception; you view them, and as you desire, you identify with them and work through them.

Now we are ready to go on to the conclusion of this practice, through the final three steps of concentration, meditation and ultimate union. The next section will complete this cycle of action.

BOOK THREE

Perfect Superconsciousness and Soul Ability

PERFECT SUPERCONSCIOUSNESS AND SOUL ABILITY

1. The Sixth Step in Proper Practice Is Concentration.

Directing the attention to one point is concentration.

2. The Seventh Step Is Meditation, or an Unbroken Flow of Attention.

3. This Leads to the Eighth and Final Step, or Identification with the Object Concentrated Upon.

4-15. These Three Stages Are Called Contemplation.

Since we will be dealing with these three stages in our discussion to follow, it will simplify things if we use the word *contemplation* to mean the gradual attainment of identification. Contemplation of anything leads to eventual realization on that level due to inner unfoldment. The object is the anchor point for consciousness and the understanding rises to the surface and is recognized. This is the natural process which we call learning, but we are dealing with it scientifically by going directly to the point. As we contemplate, the surface activity of the mind settles down, and as this happens, pure truth dawns. Though this may seem difficult in the beginning, habit will make it easy to experience.

When all mental activity is stilled, serene superconscious awareness emerges. As the activity of the mind gives us the picture of time, space and manifold situations; in the superconscious state we transcend time, space and circumstances, and we see the Real behind the unreal. Thus we are liberated. *We are liberated not as a reward, but as a consequence of realization.*

16. By Contemplation on Change Comes the Realization Concerning Time.

We now begin to deal with the transformation of mental powers. While it is true that the highest goal is to rest in superconsciousness, when we choose to function on this or any other plane, it is good to be able to understand our surroundings. The truth about time is that time does not pass, and there is no past or future in reality. There is *now,* and with this vision comes the fourth dimensional realization. Events and levels of consciousness are existing now. As we move from event to event, from viewpoint to viewpoint, we have the experience of time passing. It is our illusion and, of course, a convenient one as long as we rest on this plane of activity. Our idea of time is related to our dimension, and we have a certain time-sense as human beings. But even this may be varied among different people, for we have the psychological aspect which enters in, and some people seem to experience time passing at a more rapid rate than others. Some people seem to have adequate time to do everything they want to do, and others never seem to find time for anything. This is largely a matter of conditioning.

People on other dimensions often experience time differently than we do, as their acceptance of it is different. When we come to the point where we transcend the time-sense but still remain embodied, then we move freely in this world, selecting our experiences at will, for we see that they already exist and have only to be claimed.

17. By Contemplation on the Intent Behind the Sound Uttered by Any Living Thing Comes the Understanding of the Intent, and the Communication with the Life Form.

This is more than telepathy. This is identification with the life essence residing in the body, whether it be human form or animal form. There need be no barrier between souls, regardless of the body form. The limitation of the physical body may prevent articulation, but the desire and intent of the soul can be discerned. Constantly practice being aware of life being what it is, regardless of the appearance.

18. By Perceiving Memories, We Gain the Realization of Past Physical Embodiments.

The memories of life on this and other planes are recorded in the subconscious and are taken from body to body. In deep meditation when the conscious mind is relaxed, past memories spring up, giving proof of psychological experiences in time and space. There is no reason for dwelling at any one point in time if the experience then seems better than now, for the memories are but recordings of past dramas. While it is true that the soul inhabits a number of bodies in succession, in order to work out or neutralize certain desire patterns, it is also true that with illumination these patterns are transcended. We do not have to look forward to a long series of physical embodiments as our destiny when we realize our real nature, *for the I AM or Master Consciousness has nothing to do with the fluctuations of consciousness and identification with the shadow world.* There is often the experience at a certain point of illumination, when the past life memories flash before the inner vision in motion picture-like sequence, and as this happens the emotional charge incidental to the memories is exploded and released. Thus, past karma or subconscious patterns are eradicated. This is an automatic process.

19-20. By Contemplating the Mind of Another Person, the Truth Concerning Him Is Revealed.

While some clairvoyants can see auras and thought forms about another person and *read* him with accuracy, the true Adept knows the truth about anyone just by looking. It is assumed that when one gets to this point of awareness, the desire to control or use another because of what is seen will be absent. It is a simple thing to know the intent and level of consciousness of another.

21-22. It Is Possible to Become *Invisible* to Ordinary Sense by Withdrawing Radiation of the Body.

Objects are seen as they *send* impulses to the eye of the beholder. By consciously withdrawing these impulses, it is possible to be ignored and overlooked. You will still be solid and real to this world, but as you send no impulses, you are not detected. Thus it is possible to hide in a crowd, and even though others about you suffer confusion and fear, you can avoid it by withholding your feelings. This does not imply control of the other person's mind.

23. Karmic Patterns Are of Two Kinds: Those to Be Manifest Immediately and Those to Be Manifest at a Later Date. By Contemplation on These Patterns It Is Possible to Know the Term of Experience in This or Any Other World.

The desire patterns are cause and the manifestation is effect. We have desire patterns which will manifest immediately because situations are open for the manifestation, and we have those which will manifest in the future when the overall life pattern is in harmony with them. By being aware of the desire patterns, it is possible to foretell the future as related to personal experience. Or by being aware of the patterns of others, it is a simple matter to foretell their future, at least as far as the present trends indicate. Karmic patterns are always subject to modification when properly understood. It is even possible to tell the precise time and manner of the soul leaving the body, for everyone has already accepted this on the unconscious level. This is because most people agree, without thinking, to the race idea of old age and death. *The true student rises in consciousness, however, and breaks this binding belief and is no longer limited by the ordinary rules.* The easiest way to extend the life experience on any plane is to project some goals, and a reason for being.

24. By Contemplation on the Qualities of Friendship and Communication with All Life Comes the Manifestation of These Qualities.

While it is conceivable that an Adept could, for the purpose of working with a certain group, manifest the qualities of dissension and bring about external unrest (with the real motive being eventual peace and harmony), it is evident that the most usual qualities manifest are the ones of the more aesthetic nature.

25. **By Contemplation on Cosmic Energy, This Energy Comes under the Conscious Direction of the Purified Mind.**

The energy lying dormant (to our human sense) in the heart of the atom can be realized, and then directed by an act of will. It goes without saying that such an exercise of will should be in line with the highest motives. This cosmic power is perceived through the practice of the technique for listening to the cosmic sound. (See Techniques.)

26. ***Contemplation of the Light Within Brings Realization of the Activity of Energy on All Levels, from Subtle to Gross Manifestations.**

Since there is only one substance, everywhere manifest, then regardless of the level of manifestation, we are dealing with the same thing. *As the awareness is extended, we can become conscious of all levels at will.*

27. **By Contemplating the Mystery of This Solar System Comes the Realization of This Universe, Inside and Out.**

The universe being a manifestation of the cosmic play of ideas is seen as seven main spheres, with which we shall deal, in descending order from subtle to gross manifestation.

Perfect Superconsciousness and Soul Ability

A. The Absolute. The plane beyond description, light, darkness or activity. This is the plane of Beingness or Isness.
B. The plane of first activity as ideas are projected from the Absolute. This level is experienced only when the weight of the mind is left behind.
C. The beginning of the consciousness of separation begins on this plane. The ideas begin to manifest independent action and have a sense of separateness due to delusion. This is required if they are to fully manifest.
D. The Cosmic Conscious level. Here is the manifestation of the atom, and the beginning of the formation of the cosmos. This taking place under the passive direction of an overriding intelligence, a projection of the Absolute. *Here we see the fusion of mind and matter, or matter as we know it, being precipitated. It should be borne in mind that an understanding of this creative process will enable the Adept to duplicate it at will, on any scale on which he chooses to operate.*
E. Next comes the plane of Mind. This is the level upon which our modern (1) Mental Scientists operate and is the most effective and practical at this time, for as we have stressed, beyond this point one may move in realization. But since the realization is beyond this world, one can only have the reflection of his realization manifest. This is good for individual realization, *but impossible to teach, except by example and personal presence.* The understanding of the mental laws will prepare a person for the next step in unfoldment. In fact, I believe this to be the logical order of unfoldment. The teachings of the mental laws will come forth to be acceptable to the masses. This will lighten

the mass consciousness and prepare the world for the Golden Age.

In this sphere we find the electricities and magnetic flows required to bind the atoms together. We also find the realization to bring this about by an act of will, or by *accepting* that it is done. Though we may exercise this ability, we do so in harmony with the overall life plan for this particular cosmos. The Adept is the channel through which the Power flows into manifestation, and wherever there is a need for this Power to manifest, there you will find instruments in the form of highly aware individuals. This is a cosmic and impersonal phenomenon. While it is true that Life uses many unknowing instruments, *It also uses conscious instruments who are the Adepts, Masters and Illuminates of the time.* (More of this in our discussion in verse 32.)

F. The second plane is the astral plane or plane of finer electricities and fine matters, which are harmoniously coordinated. There is an astral pattern existing behind every physical manifestation, for every physical manifestation is the projection of pure consciousness; it cannot exist alone. We shall discuss the astral plane in verse 30 of this chapter.

G. The full projection results in the physical world as we see it with ordinary vision. Now it is possible to detach the consciousness from this body and from this world and be aware of other planes of consciousness, and the techniques set forth in this book will make it possible. Regardless of whether or not you wear a body on this or any other plane, it is possible to come to the full realization of the Superconscious State.

28-29. Contemplation of the Moon and Pole-star Brings Knowledge of the Stars, Their Groupings and Motions.

As the attention is directed to the heavenly bodies, there arises an understanding of their properties and motions, based on fixed laws and electrical activities. With this insight comes an automatic understanding of the influence of the heavenly bodies on the physical bodies on the planet earth. It is revealed how all parts of creation are linked together and interchange their influences. The influences emitted by any body in this creation are neither good nor bad, merely active. When they mingle with the patterns of other bodies, then harmony or chaos ensues, but through no conscious motive on the part of any force or radiation. Man reacts to impartial radiations according to his desire pattern and his subconscious conditioning. While it is true that man, bodily identified, is influenced by everything else in this world, including the planets, when he comes into conscious realization of his Soul Awareness, he slips free from all bondage because he is no longer attuned to the activities of this world. The electrical and magnetic radiations circulate constantly throughout the universe. The average man is completely influenced by these radiations. The fully aware man becomes cause and emits his own radiation, becoming a center of power, rather than a victim of cosmic energies.

Since there are no accidents in this or any other world, the man is fortunate who learns to attune himself with the activity of life on all levels. Even the radiations of the stars are the activity of Spirit, stepped down in frequency and moving with unconscious purpose, to keep creation balanced and in existence.

There are numberless planets in space suited for physical habitation, but regardless of the level of consciousness of the race located on a specific planet, it is a fallacy to assume that they are *ahead* of us in any great sense. It may be that certain planets in space are at the peak of the golden age, while we are still in the early stages of the ascending cycle; but we have a few men who have come to the level of Adeptship, and regardless of where the body happens to be in space, and regardless of the particular planet, a pure level of consciousness is the same. Thus an Adept on the planet Earth would be equal in consciousness, and therefore understanding, to an Adept on a planet in this or any other solar system. It is a mistake to assume that man on this planet is backward and crude because of his ignorance. We are in our present situation because we are just coming out of the dark ages and ascending into a period of unfoldment that will culminate in the golden age, about the year A.D. 12,500.

We are at present 261 years into the ascending electrical age. Let us see how we arrive at this conclusion. We learn from our references to Oriental astronomy that moons revolve around their planets, and planets turning on their axes, revolve with their moons around the sun; and the sun, taking some distant body in space, revolves about it. This takes about 24,000 years, and it is this celestial phenomenon which causes the backward movement of the equinoctial points around the zodiac. But there is a deeper significance. The sun also revolves about a magnetic center and *this movement about the magnetic center effects a subtle influence on the perceptual ability of humans on this planet.* When the sun in its movement comes to the nearest point to this magnetic center, the veil of perception is so thinned that the average

Perfect Superconsciousness and Soul Ability

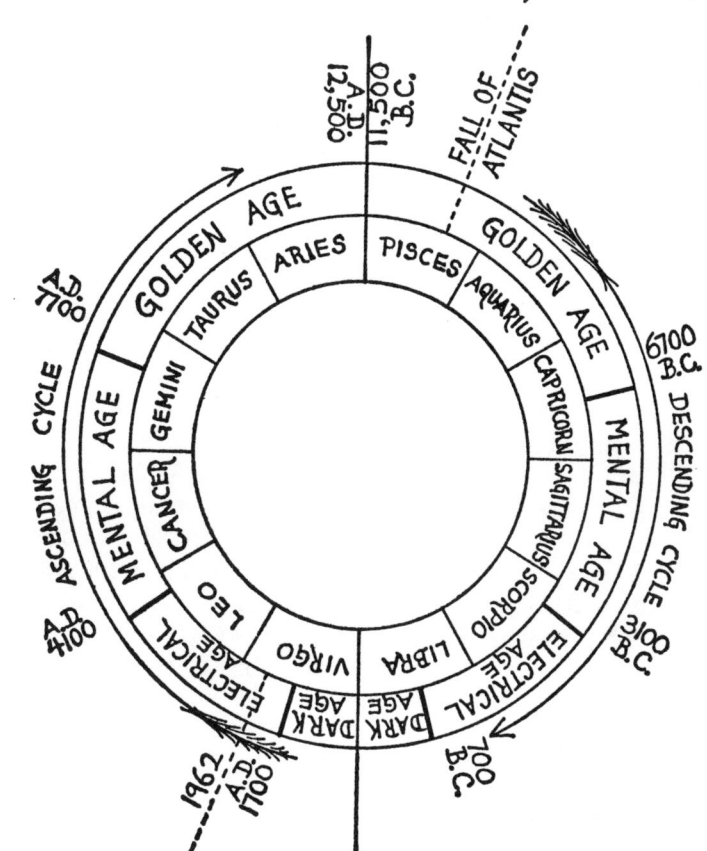

man can intuitively know truth. At this time, civilization has a golden age.

Then, 12,000 years later, the sun is at the point farthest from this magnetic center, and at this time the veil is so dense that the average man can only be aware of this material level of creation. We must bear in mind, however, that regardless of the astronomical situation, there are always a few men who have transcended this influence, and rest in the recognition of their Spiritual nature. The time when the sun is nearest to the magnetic center is when the autumnal equinox comes to the first point of Aries. When the sun is farthest away, the autumnal equinox is on the first point of Libra.

During this grand 24,000 year cycle, there is a complete alteration in both the material and intellectual world, as the material world is governed by the intellectual world. From the low point when the ascending cycle of 12,000 years begins, we see a gradual but sure unfoldment of the consciousness of man. This takes place in four progressive stages. The first 1,200 years are the dark ages when the mind is at the lowest ebb. The second stage of 2,400 years is the electrical age when man is capable of perceiving the electricities and finer forces of nature. The third stage of 3,600 years is the mental age, and man is then able to comprehend the world of mind and the fusion of higher and lower frequencies. The final 4,800 years leads into the peak of the golden age when man is wide awake as far as his spiritual nature is concerned. Then begins the descent, following the reverse pattern of ascent, and in the same time segments, until the cycle reaches the bottom and 24,000 years is complete. Then the process begins anew, each time the high point being a bit higher than the previous high, and the low point being a bit higher than the previous time, so

Perfect Superconsciousness and Soul Ability

that we see the overall pattern is one of refinement of this solar system and a quickening of the basic substance. *It is quite conceivable that in due time this solid earth will fade from view and continue on in another dimension—real to the inhabitants but no longer visible to other space beings who will then rest in our present state of unfoldment.* At the peak of the golden age, advanced souls incarnate to gain experience, and when the pattern begins to descend, they move on to other planets or planes where they can express, while souls whose karmic patterns are in harmony with existing conditions will incarnate at the suitable time. Civilization does not rise or fall with the whims of man, but man does unfold in consciousness or fall into ignorance (as a species, but not as an individual) as the cosmic cycle moves on.

Now if this be true, it should be observable in this world. Let us see whether it is or not. According to astronomical calculations, the time when the sun reached the closest point to the magnetic center was 11,500 B.C., and at that time the sun began its move from the center and the intellectual powers of man began to diminish. While recorded history at this time does not go back before 3,500 B.C. we do have the verbal accounts preserved through myths and stories of golden age activities. It is interesting to note that Plato in the *Critias* describes a golden age with the focal point in Atlantis. The government was controlled by a group of Philosopher Kings and it was a philosophic democracy. The arts flourished and the sciences were cultivated in great universities. Men had no enemies and war was unknown. Gradually, however, their divine consciousness began to fade away and they lost their spiritual virtues. Personal ambition increased and corruption ensued. Atlantis fell and the consciousness of mankind continued to spiral downward with the move of the descending cycle. It is recorded that Atlantis fell about 9,000 years before the siege of Troy, which was about 184 B.C.—thus we see the fall of Atlantis was during the descending golden age about the year 10,184 B.C. or about 1,316 years after it had begun to descend in following the pattern of the sun moving away from the magnetic center. From that point on, the rapid decline is evident in our records until it reached the bottom of the cycle about A.D. 499 at which time it began to rise. The dark ages were at their worst at the bottom the the cycle.

Atlantis fell beneath the waves of the Atlantic in a great turmoil. The glory that was hers lingered on, however, because the poets and philosophers who had been there carried on the story. Even in the dark ages, truth is not lost, for there are always a few who are able to transcend time and space, and perceive Reality. The techniques and arts are passed on through word of mouth, and veiled in symbolic writings and architecture. There is always a band of illumined souls whose work it is to preserve wisdom for the ages. Now in this 261st year (1961) of the electrical age, we find the need for symbology dropping away as the mass consciousness is able to discern the truth openly. The bars of secrecy are being removed and greater numbers of advancing souls admitted to the inner temple. It is highly probable that Atlantis had the secret of aerial locomotion and an understanding of directing nature's powers, such as we are capable of doing now. This also is to be found in the ancient tales that have come down through the ages. For as Plato talked of the fall of Atlantis, so the *Mahabharata,* an epic poem of India, tells of an ancient war between the good and evil powers, personalized as bodies of men, and in these tales are to be found the evidence of flying machines and weapons capable of directing terrific quantities of energy.

The 12,000 years of the ascending and descending arcs are broken up into four stages of 1,200, 2,400, 3,600, and 4,800 years respectively, starting with the dark ages. The decline follows the reverse pattern. Each age is at its fullest in the middle of the stage, and the beginnings and endings are periods of overlapping and merging, which is evident in the gradualness of emerging truths in the ascending cycle and the gradualness of the dimming of mass consciousness in the descending cycle. (Observe this in the chart.) The understanding of this cosmic, but natural, process insures peace of mind as the assurance that an enlightened civilization is coming into expression. We can now relieve ourselves of worry and fear when we view the stumbling attempts of modern man to help himself. It is impossible for man to fall from his destiny, and as we rise into the new age we find that according to ancient prophecy, now coming true, that North America is destined to be the center of golden age activity.

30. Contemplation at the Center of the Body Brings Knowledge of the Nature and Condition of the Body.

As one concentrates with an open mind on the nature of the body, there comes the realization of the nature of the body, not only the vital centers through which life forces are directed, but the various energies, electricities and mental attributes that go to make up the body. Also revealed, is the nature of the desire patterns which are the cause of this body's existence on this plane.

The astral body, which survives physical experience is energy, held together by crystallized ideas, which make up the mental body. These thirty-five ideas are the basic pattern from which is formed the subtle astral body of nineteen elements and the physical body of sixteen elements. The nineteen elements of the astral body are mental, emotional and lifetronic. The nineteen components are intelligence; ego; (idea of separateness from Spirit) feeling; mind; five instruments of knowledge, the counterparts of the senses of sight, hearing, smell, taste, touch, five instruments of action, the mental correspondence for the executive abilities to procreate, excrete, talk, walk and exercise manual ability; and the five instruments of life force, empowered to perform the crystallizing, assimilating, eliminating, metabolizing and circulating functions of the body. The sixteen elements of the physical body are metallic and nonmetallic.

Though there is a universal pattern for human bodies on this planet, the body is modified according to certain desire patterns and psychological distortions. When conception takes place, the soul makes contact with the fertilized egg, and as the astral body is vibrating with unfulfilled desires and subconscious patterns, the body that is formed in the mother's womb takes the human body form because of the genetic pattern, but is modified with characteristics brought from previous experiences. We are a mixture of the total race memory due to the body given by our parents, and we add to this the total of our own memories in other bodies in other times and spaces. Our parents, as well as the geographical location in which we are born, is predestined by our desires and our need for unfulfilled desires to have a channel for expression.

The mental, astral and physical bodies are connected at centers where the vital forces interpenetrate. The most common of these centers are the main nerve centers in

Perfect Superconsciousness and Soul Ability

the spine and brain, although there are centers all over the body. The even flow of life energy keeps the astral body functioning perfectly. Just as the circulation of blood is important for the physical body, so the flow of life force is important for the astral or energy body. In fact there are cases on record of men and women so aware of their astral bodies, while encased in physical bodies, that the vitality radiates through the physical body and they do not have to eat as we know it, and they are not subject to the laws of diet, sleep or exercise. It is because they are aware on a deeper level. The more we become aware of the astral body and the flow of life force, the less dependent we are on the physical world.

Students of the occult are aware of the main centers in the body. The spine is a very important part of the anatomy, for it is here that the rush of Spirit is first evident as it pours into the body to be directed throughout the body on all levels. Energy flows down from the brain after it enters at the medulla oblongata, is split into dual polarity, and is directed from the third eye center in the forehead. There is an automatic direction of force from this control center. The energy is directed down the spine and at the various centers; cervical, dorsal, lumbar, sacral and coccygeal, the energy is directed into the body and altered in frequency to take care of the needs of the body. We will discuss this on the three levels, starting from the bottom of the spine and moving upward.

Coccygeal Plexus —Located at the base of the spine— has the vibration that maintains the solidity of the body and the cohesion of the atomic structure. Nerves here carry the energy which supplies the organs in the pelvic region.

Sacral Plexus	—Located up the spine a few inches—has the vibration that maintains the fluid balance in the body.
Lumbar Plexus	—Located in the spine opposite the navel. Connected with the solar plexus. Produces heat—psychic and physical. It is known as the fire center.
Dorsal Plexus	—In the spine between the shoulder blades—intimately connected with the cardiac nerves. Astral function is to control the movement of vital airs in the body.
Cervical Plexus	—In spine opposite the throat. Astral function is to maintain the balance of the ethers in the sub-atomic spaces of the body. It is at this center that one concentrates to learn to feed the body with lifetrons or subtle life force.
Third Eye Center	—Point between the eyebrows. The center of conscious will, and center of unconscious (automatic) control of life forces in the body. Attention centered here in meditation draws relaxed energies to this point. Lifts consciousness from idea of duality to realization of oneness. Not a mental state, but an actual realization.
Mid-Brain	—Body battery and storage area for cosmic energy in the body. Consciousness realized here is unconditioned. Absolute awareness. Pure Beingness.

It must be realized that we are not concerned with getting lost in a maze of intricate technicalities. We are concerned with understanding the nature of the body and how consciousness is condensed as the body. The step-by-step process is interesting to understand. As we identify with the various centers of consciousness, we manifest our state of awareness on this plane. A person who is attuned to the coccygeal plexus is aware of the external world as the only reality. Naturally, his actions are motivated from this point of view. When the consciousness identifies with the sacral center, we find a little awakening take place; man begins to feel the stirring of the Spirit within. It is in the nature of an impulse. This begins the search for Self, which will take many turns on the path, unless the individual is blessed with high realization from previous incarnations; and if this is the case, he will find himself propelled effortlessly to make the right contacts and avoid the pitfalls of diversion, which would delay his unfoldment. He begins to get *hunches* or intuitional glimpses, but lacks understanding of what is happening.

When the consciousness identifies and works through the lumbar center, we find the individual at the turning point in the spiritual life. Here we find a deep feeling, almost a certainty, of the subtle life, and yet an attachment because of long experience to the belief in a three-dimensional, solid universe. Here we find more vivid experiences to indicate the awakening, such as precognitive dreams or visions, manifestations of extra-sensory perception, though uncontrolled, and a more obvious interest in the deeper things of life. If we remain steady, then we experience the opening of consciousness at the dorsal center. With this experience comes the realization of our subtle nature and of the activities of feelings and forces within our bodies and in the world around us. It is common to experience a communion with nature at this point of unfoldment. When the consciousness works through the cervical center, we find peace of mind and mental balance. It is easier to be at peace when the realization of life is experienced and when we understand the nature of life activity.

When the consciousness works through the third eye center or center of will, we are free while expressing in this world. We let the energies in the body do their work, and we maintain a proper balance with life, but we operate from a higher center; and though we appear to be active in this world, we are not influenced by anything that takes place about us. We get into communication with people and circumstances, but we do not get involved to the point where we are controlled and lose our balance. We do not create compulsive desire patterns and we cannot experience bondage for our actions. *When we move intuitively, we move by grace, and whatever we do is automatically right for the time and place.* As an instrument for the universal Life, we are removed from personal responsibility.

When the awareness is established in the midbrain, we have continuous realization of the Absolute, either in meditation, or while performing ordinary duties. This is an unbroken realization, and the person who experiences this can wear a body, or do as he will, and there is nothing that can touch, or hinder him. He moves as spirit, without restriction of any kind.

It often happens that while the realization of the Absolute is actual, there appears to be a conflict in the body behaviour and condition. Let us look at the various levels of awareness. After the superconscious state is attained and can be maintained continuously, it still remains for the body to be regenerated. It still remains for the pure awareness to work itself down into the body and purify

Perfect Superconsciousness and Soul Ability

the body of flesh, energy and mental patterns. There are individuals who attain a high level of consciousness, but who do not purify the body, and they either leave the body at transition, or through error re-identify with them, and experience a gradual, but usually temporary, eclipse of Absolute awareness. An individual who is aware of superconsciousness at all times but is still working out on this plane, the desire patterns created in the past, is called *the living free*. The consciousness is clear, but the body is dissolving the existing desire patterns. This accounts for adverse body conditions in highly aware souls. However, it is my thought that we should bring the superconscious awareness down into the body and purify the body on all levels. We must bear in mind, however, that we must leave the blueprint for the body on the subconscious level, otherwise the body would disintegrate.

It is not enough merely to stir up the energies and produce psychic manifestations, and dramatizations of desires. It is important to cleanse the body on all levels, while at the same time, acting from the highest impulses. The awakening activity can bring on a variety of manifestations according to the quality of the mind. (See chart of mental qualities.)

There are various grades of liberation of which the state of the *living free* is but one. With the complete realization of cosmic consciousness, and the intent to move in that consciousness, comes the state of being supremely free. A soul which is supremely free can act as a god, for this is the nature of a god. Spirit does not act except through instruments. A supremely liberated soul is the highest and purest instrument for the flow of Power. Such a one can create and disperse universes, take on one or any number of bodies in this time and space, or any other time and space, and operate them simultaneously.

They are the Masters and Adepts, and their status and behaviour bear no resemblance to the imagined characters fictionalized in popular religious texts by well-meaning but deluded writers, who simply project their own mental images in their writings and create glorified kings and rulers. The Masters have nothing to do with this kind of fantasy.

The physical body is purified as the pure consciousness comes to the surface. The vibrations are elevated and there is the quickening of vital forces at the same time, for it is inconceivable that one body at a time would be acted upon. The choice of food, pleasure and activity may alter as this action takes place. The desires are purified. This does not mean that you will not have desire, for desire is necessary for expression on this level, but the desires will be expressions of natural impulses and not perversions of them, due to distorted mental images or restlessness. The mental body will be cleansed as the compulsive desires and negative emotional conditions are erased. The overall effect will be one of extreme well being and buoyancy. It is not inconceivable that the body would eventually be dispersed at will at the time of transition, for all that would have to take place would be a release of the cohesive force and the energy particles making up the body would scatter, and the body would be no more. *The only thing that holds the body together is desire for expression, and this causes energy particles to form about the matrix of the body and manifest as a body on whatever plane the soul's desire pattern is attuned.*

It is possible, at a certain level of awareness, to erase the desire patterns and emotional patterns by projecting them on the vision level. The fully aware individual sits quietly and goes into the silence. Becoming aware of the desire patterns and their need to be expressed or erased,

Perfect Superconsciousness and Soul Ability 105

he will then project himself in a conscious dream (really an astral level) and fulfill the desires in order to exhaust them, thus doing away with them in short order and with full control. The average person can do this to a degree, with the technique of revision.

The individual can help to purify the body on all levels by making a conscious attempt to keep the body clean and in good working order, and by endeavoring to be motivated properly, and by keeping the emotional life in order. This is all helped greatly by the exercise of high level conversation and activity. All our conscious efforts will not gain us any merit, but they will render the body and mind a fit instrument for a greater inflow of the Spirit.

A person who has full awareness of his true nature can maintain a body on this level for as long as he wishes. With the realization of the Spiritual nature comes the release from the delusions of the limited vision. There is no scientific reason for the body to grow old and fade away. There are masters today who keep their bodies in perfect condition, in the prime of life from the casual viewpoint, yet they have had these bodies for several hundreds of years. This is not an exaggeration. They maintain their state of physical well being because they have the realization that the body is a condensed thought, and if the mental image is that of youth and health, then the body as the outpicturing of the mental image will be manifest on this level accordingly. This is not brought about by using affirmations, or auto-conditioning techniques; *but it is the direct result of resting in the pure recognition of the true nature of the body.*

The soul inhabits and operates a body which is a suitable instrument and which is adapted to the environment in which it desires to express. It is conceivable that bodies on other planets may differ from our body form, because of the organism's need to adapt to atmospheric pressures and other local phenomena. It is not important to worry about the superior state of beings on other planets, because it is a matter of consciousness. Since there are countless solar systems, then it stands to reason that there are many planets in space now supporting intelligent life. There are planets with life manifesting at different phases —some where the organisms are just beginning to be active and others where they are manifesting the golden age. This may lead to some speculation as to how man came to be on this planet. There are many theories and, of course, it is not necessary to assume that there is a plan for populating all planets in the same way. I think it is quite obvious that the physical body containing within it, as it does, the intricate control centers and deepseated reaction patterns, is the product of evolution. I did not say that the soul awakening is a matter of evolution. *There are at least two paths here.*

Bodies evolve as they adapt to their environment and as the urge of the soul nature pushes outward. So we have a dual action taking place—the need to adapt to a threatening environment, and the innate desire for soul to express through the instrument. This inner pushing, as it were, causes a refining process to take place on the one hand, and is also the reason for souls leaving bodies in order to reincarnate in bodies that meet their unfolding needs. While identified with a body that does not contain the intricate nervous system, the soul is limited as the perception is filtered through the subconscious of the organism. In order to find free expression on earth, the soul needs a human body, equipped as it is, with the cerebro-spinal nervous system. In the human body we find the most perfect instrument on the planet for expression. It is possible with self-consciousness and the use of certain techniques, to refine the body even further and open up new areas of consciousness, and thus bring it into such a state that it allows for the free flow of Spirit. Lower life forms, while being operated by life units or souls, do not have the potential to be refined. It may offend the sensibilities of some people to think of animals as having souls, but we are concerned here not with argument, but with facts as they appear to be.

While there is no reason to believe that the present human form is not the product of evolution (and the inner unfoldment), it is also quite conceivable that the planet was visited at some remote time and the visitors remained and intermarried with the then highest life forms, the result being a great step forward in the time sense, of bringing man into his present state. There is also the reference in ancient scriptures of *divine beings* emerging to this vibratory frequency to mate with the then highest life forms, and the result being the same. Either from other planets or from other planes, the effect would be the quickening of evolution as we know it, as bodies were prepared to house souls of higher awareness. This is always the need—bodies sufficiently equipped to be used for fully aware souls.

When souls no longer desire to function on this level, they move on to some other. There is no need to remain with one planet forever. This planet is following a definite upward pattern and will have its fulfillment in time, just as will the souls who choose to inhabit it.

31-32. By Fixing the Consciousness in the Area of the Cervical Center Comes Control of Hunger, and Poise of Body.

As mentioned in the previous commentary, when the understanding in relationship to the cervical center is opened, then it is actually possible to overcome hunger, either by supplying the body with life force or by shutting off artificial cravings. This also relates to other hungers, the hungers of compulsively motivated desire. When the consciousness is established at this point, the life forces are controlled and the mental attitude detached. This enables one to be poised and objective.

33. By Becoming Conscious of the Light in the Head One Can Also Learn to See the Masters and Adepts.

Not only does this level of consciousness enable a person to recognize an Adept on this plane, but to *see* them on other planes through clairvoyant vision. It seems paradoxical that before one can recognize an Adept, one must lift the consciousness to the point where the truth can be perceived. There are an infinite number of dimensions existing *here* in space, filled with all manner of embodied souls. Through clairvoyant vision it is possible to part the curtain and attune to the desired level. Negative people contact the dregs of the astral as their perceptions quicken, restless people contact others like themselves, who have gone on into the astral but who are not any more illumined. Pure minded individuals contact illumined beings, on this and other planes. This is possible when the barrier of time and space ceases to exist. Usually we will contact an Adept in deep meditation, when we *tune out* this world, although it is possible to see through the veil into their realm of activity while being fully aware of this world. Since we are sensitized by contacting the light within, *we become aware of the subtle worlds already existing about us.*

This ability has nothing to do with ordinary phases of mediumship or with a glorified system of heavenly rulers

Perfect Superconsciousness and Soul Ability

working through instruments. It is true that certain Adepts desire to carry out their work and will impress their intention upon someone on this plane who is a fit instrument, but such direction is reserved for those who have prepared themselves, and always builds the person, never depletes or destroys. The Adepts do not need to enslave people to work for them.

Masters and Adepts usually work through individuals who are attuned to them and who have worked with them in the past. Usually when an Adept incarnates, he brings with him a band of helpers to carry out the work. Even when the Adept leaves this plane, he can still inspire and guide his disciples in the right direction. This usually takes place through inspiration. That is, the disciple is inspired to move in a certain way according to his own talents. Adepts do not meddle in the private affairs of people. Instances of so-called Adepts speaking through students in trance, to the detriment of the students' health and mental well-being, is a travesty of this relationship. An illumined Master does not need to be at the beck and call of an emotionally unstable medium.

The safest method of practice is to sit in the silence and become aware of cosmic consciousness, and in this high state, let the experiences come. To seek a contact out of desperation will in most instances bring about only a projection of a subconscious desire, and such self-deception is a hindrance on the path.

34. Steady Meditation Leads to Spontaneous Enlightenment and Pure Vision.

As steady contemplation leads ultimately to identification with the object contemplated, so steady meditation will eventually bring the experience of transcendental vision. This takes place when all thoughts are brought to a standstill and the attention is shifted from the body and body associations, to the realization of pure consciousness, which does not need a body to exist. When there is a free flow of awareness through the sense centers of the body, you will have conscious awareness of the cosmic. With this enlightenment comes instant realization of the unity of the cosmic activity, and the realization that there is but one body, the cosmic body. With complete identification and pure vision, comes the knowledge of the eternal nature of Spirit and Soul, which is an individualization of Spirit.

35. Contemplation on the Heart Center Brings Knowledge of the Realm of Mind.

In the creative process, unconditioned consciousness steps down through various phases and one phase is the level of mind. Just as there is the individualization of mind in man, so there is the universal mind, graded as it were, to handle creative processes. When we concentrate on the heart center, which has been termed the door to the inner kingdom, we experience the unfoldment of awareness and gain the realization of the ocean of mind, in which everything is floating. As in a large body of water there can exist an infinite number of forms made of ice, some hard, some soft, yet all formed of the water and in the water, so in the ocean of mind there exists an infinite number of forms, varying in degree of density, yet formed of, and existing in, the ocean of mind. The thing we must grasp is that *everything is consciousness in form, and besides this, there is nothing.* Everything is created from the same basic cause substance, and has its reality only be-

Perfect Superconsciousness and Soul Ability 111

cause of this fact. It is impossible to have any part of creation break off and be other than consciousness. It may seem that at times some people seem to believe they are separate due to ego consciousness, but such is not the case, as they will one day realize. Since everyone and everything is consciousness in form, then nothing can be lost, *and in the absolute sense there is no diminishing or increasing of universal substance.*

Understanding the nature of universal mind, it is a simple thing to understand the mental activity of human beings.

36. Inability to Accept the Vision of a Non-dual World Leads to Confusion. On the Other Hand, Recognition of Spirit Solves All Problems.

Lack of discrimination, or lack of ability to tell truth from untruth, is the reason for all human misery. Such a situation is resolved as the light of truth dawns. It is a mistake to assume that one has to *work out* certain karmic patterns and project the idea into the future. When the light dawns, the past is wiped out, regardless of what the past has been. Many people find it extremely difficult to accept the fact that what they see as confusion and unhappiness, exists, and they feel guilty at the idea of transcending this level. Yet every soul goes through the phase of experiencing misery due to misunderstanding; and for the awakening soul to wallow in misery just because others do not seem to get the point is to slow the unfolding experience. As we are all connected in truth, then my realization of truth will automatically help others to rise in consciousness, and the best thing I can do for others is to experience cosmic consciousness.

37. Along with Spontaneous Enlightenment Comes Realization of Truth on Various Levels, Manifesting Through the Senses of Hearing, Touching, Seeing, Tasting and Smelling.

When we experience partial enlightenment, we find that since we are still oriented to the body, we perceive through the sense channels. Now it is not necessary to work through the channel of the senses, but being only partially illumined, we do begin to see the manifestations. This is known as clairvoyant perception when manifesting through the sense of sight; clairaudient perception when manifesting through the sense of hearing. What is happening is that we are perceiving intuitively, yet not clearly, so we use the sense channels. As we do this we are also likely to experience imperfect sensing, as the body patterns and subconscious conditionings act as filters through which the sensing flows, and at times it is distorted.

38. These Experiences Are Obstacles to Liberation, but in the Ordinary Sense They Are Powers Which Come Through Enlightenment.

Let us understand these powers, for the next few verses will go into them in detail. It is a frustrating experience for a person to suddenly awaken to the realization of these powers and then be told that they stand in the way of liberation. In fact, this is such a shock to many people that they think at this point they know more than the teacher and decide to go their way alone. This usually ends in disaster, or at least it ends in the student becoming so confused by the maze of psychic activity that he becomes totally bewildered.

Perfect Superconsciousness and Soul Ability 113

As it is obvious that even the most enlightened cannot sit in a high state of ecstasy all of the time, but must work through the body, it is important to come to an understanding of these powers. These powers properly used from the viewpoint of highest intuition, can be the means of great blessing. *A point to clear up right here is that there is no harm in using these powers for constructive purposes, for it is the nature of the soul to gain greater ability as it unfolds.* It is only when the powers are used selfishly that trouble comes, but then this happens on any plane. There is nothing to be afraid of as long as you operate from a high level of consciousness. Of course some superstitious people will arch their eyebrows and appear wise in their pronouncements against the use of these powers for any occasion, but we will have nothing of such smallness in our present discussion. *The reason why the powers serve as obstacles on the path is that students tend to become fascinated by them, and forget the real goal of life.* An understanding of these powers, used in their proper place, is helpful and practical.

A Commentary on the Powers

39. **When the Cause of the Mind Being Attached to a Specific Body Is Understood and There Is Realization of the Nervous System Through Which the Life Forces Flow, Then It Is Possible to Withdraw from the Body at Will and Even Enter the Body of Another.**

As the soul is free when properly aware, so it can move from a body consciously if it desires to do so. This is accomplished by understanding the process of how the mental, astral and physical bodies are joined. There is a technique (see second Kriya) whereby the advanced student leaves the body by withdrawing the life current through the spinal centers, these being the points where the vital forces are attached to the body. It is also theoretically possible to re-enter the body as long as there is a spark of life left in the nervous system.

Though there have been apparent cases of possession, where an entity with a knowledge of this process has taken over the body of a passive person, in most cases this is due to the influence of the lower nature of the person's own subconscious mind taking over, rather than an actual case of possession. Highly aware souls seldom work through the body of another, but instead they inspire telepathically, providing the person who is to be the instrument is sensitive enough to cooperate. This happens only if there is a tie between the Adept and the disciple. Adepts do not concern themselves with controlling the actions of people on this plane who do not desire such guidance. And even in cases where there is full cooperation between Adept and disciple, the Adept inspires, but the disciple is left to work out the situation according to his inner guidance and natural talent. A true Adept is not concerned with having disciples on this plane sacrifice their unfolding pattern just to carry out his personal desires. An Adept works with disciples who are in tune, and in agreement with, his plans and ideas.

The problem arises in this work when well-meaning persons, lacking true realization, assume to interpret the role of the Adept. Then they usually project a fantastic system of planetary control and an elaborate method of unfoldment, which sounds attractive to the new student, but has no basis in fact. A point to remember is, that conscious mind interpretation of the inner activity, results in incorrect analysis. This is revealed in the unsettled lives of those who indulge in such pastimes.

40. By Controlling the Life Current Regulating the Vital Airs in the Body, It Is Possible to Levitate and Leave the Body at Will.

By understanding the nature of the life current controlling the activity of the lungs and upper body parts, the true practitioner of this science can experience levitation of the body. This happens either consciously or spontaneously. Many persons have been seen in levitation, usually while in a devotional state of mind.

Also, by controlling this life current, it is possible to will the stopping of the heart and keep the body in a magnetized state so it does not suffer from this suspension of activity. A forced stopping of the heart or interference of the circulatory system would cause damage to brain cells, but in the deep state of meditation, there is an electrification of the brain cells and entire nervous system. The most important significance is that when a person arrives at this state of awareness, he is *lifted* above the attachment to the things of this world and rests in the realization of Spirit.

41. By Bringing the Vital Body to the Surface the Aspirant Is Filled with Light.

Through deep contemplation of the Life within, there is an awakening and manifesting of vital force, which, when activated, moves through the body and quickens the body on every level. At times, a light can be seen around the physical body of a person who is thus awakened, because the vitality radiates in all directions from the center. At this stage the person concerned can easily see the light within, in meditation, and has the realization that the entire body from head to toe is filled with light. So intense does this experience become, that it often seems as though even the physical body is composed of light (which indeed it is) and that one moves in a universe of light, even on this plane. The realization of this light regenerates the body and brings it to a high level of awareness. This is helpful, for it means that the bodies of the children of such parents will be sensitive and this will elevate the entire human race. As we go forward in the ascending cycle, the bodies of men and women will be purified, and this will be helpful for the highly aware souls which incarnate.

42. By Listening Deeply Within We Come to the Realization of the Eternal Sound.

In the process of listening in the silence we go through several phases. We hear in the beginning, the sounds of the physical body, then the electricities on the astral level, then we intuitively know the desire patterns, and eventually we become aware of the cosmic sound, which if contemplated, leads to eventual realization of pure consciousness. (See technique for listening to the Cosmic Sound.)

43. By Contemplating the Nature of the Levels of Creation and the Relationship of Soul to Body, Comes the Ability to Transcend Time, Space and Circumstance.

Knowing how Life acts upon itself to bring forth creation, and knowing the method of detaching from the body, the soul stands free of all limitation. The soul can operate through a body and use it according to its desire to carry out specific things on this plane, but it is not bound to this plane. This realization is a natural result of enlightenment.

44. By Steady Contemplation on the Light Which Is Beyond Form Comes Illumination.

Illumination comes quickly or in a series of quick awakenings. It is not the result of developing or acquiring knowledge, but is a severing of the connection with the body and a realization of pure awareness. In complete illumination there is no awareness of any kind of body, physical, energy or mental. There is a release into the vastness and limitlessness of Spirit. The energies from the soul are directed through the control centers of the body in order to operate the body. In most cases, however, the soul awareness is lost and only the awareness of the body remains. When this release comes, either quickly as in some cases of illumination, or in a series of awakenings, we have realization. The proof that it is realization, and not self-deception due to contact with the low astral, is that in the former there will be a feed-down of power and great perception of truth, while in the latter there tends to be an unsettling of the nervous system and a confusion of the mind.

45. By Contemplating the Nature of the Elements and Their Qualities Comes Mastery of Them.

As the understanding opens it is natural to see into the heart of nature and see exactly how things are made. There is but one substance, everywhere present, but the intricate process of creation is still taking place as the law of diversification continues. With the inner unfoldment and the understanding of the nature of the body, comes the automatic understanding of the other life forms. The secret of understanding anything is to direct the attention to it and hold steadfast until identification takes place, then there is knowledge based on the fact that you are looking *from that point* which you wished to understand. Being there, with full awareness, you naturally understand everything about the thing. Try to see the impulse behind creation and be aware of the activity and movement of energies and balancing forces that are necessary to bring the formless Light into form on the screen of space. First there is the impulse moving through a pattern, and everything else happens after that.

46. Through Complete Realization of the Nature of the Elements and Their Qualities Comes Other Powers.

We are still dealing with the function of life forces, and the perceptions as filtered through the body, and in this light we come to the eight perfections or psychic powers which are detailed in this treatise.

These powers are:

(1) *Minuteness.* The power of identifying with the smallest unit of matter in the universe. This is because the soul has the ability to identify with the object of contemplation; and if a person contemplates the atom, then this will be the realization when the contemplation has been successful. Bear in mind that this realization will be complete and that there will be complete knowledge of the atom and what takes place within it.

(2) *Magnitude.* The power of filling all space and of feeling that everything contained within this expansion

Perfect Superconsciousness and Soul Ability

is the solid body. There is the awareness of everything being one body, though many things are taking place within the body. This is true cosmic consciousness. Enlightenment is release from centers of control and means liberation, but cosmic consciousness is just what it implies.

(3) *Gravity.* Understanding the attracting force in nature and bringing it into play makes it possible to make anything, including the body, as heavy as desired. This is done with an act of will which controls the flow of subtle force.

(4) *Lightness.* Just the opposite of the above. By understanding the radiating force in nature it is possible to render any object, including the body, as weightless as desired. This is accomplished by neutralizing the attracing force.

(5) *The Attainment of Any Objective.* A true Adept with full realization should be able to do whatever he feels led to do. An understanding of the laws of nature makes it possible to fall into line with creative energies. Also an enlightened mind is free of the beliefs of failure, and the fears of attainment.

(6) *An Irresistible Will.* This will is not to be confused with blind will, but is due to the realization that the power of the universe is behind everything that is done, as long as it is consistent with the highest principle. This is the drive that enables an Adept to forge ahead once he is sure he is right, and demands the satisfaction of all desire.

(7) *Creative Power.* Just as a person on this plane can function fully on this plane if he understands the laws of the creative process, so whatever the area of awareness, the truly realized soul can operate there. In the instance of a person being aware of a large space, including several

solar systems (see No. 2 above) it is conceivable that the creation and dissolution of a group of planetary bodies would be possible. Remember, if the consciousness embraces the area of activity, then the area of command increases.

(8) *The Power to Command or Bring Anything Under Control.* By operating from the level of holding forth patterns for the universal substance to flow through, the Adept causes things to happen on any level according to his desire. It is not an effort process, but a matter of standing in the pure recognition that *it is done.* Even though the Adept assumes the station of holding forth the pattern through which the substance flows, he still remains aware of the fact that it is the Power that does everything, even forms his body and causes his mind to function. So it is not that an Adept usurps the power from the Absolute, but he is so identified with It that his actions are the results of universal desire and there is complete harmony in the behaviour pattern of the Adept, and an understanding and a working with the cosmic law.

Now it must be realized that often these powers awaken in people who have not yet learned to manifest the elevating quality. (See chart on the three qualities.) And when this happens we see:

A. In the case of people who are manifesting the destructive quality, an interest in learning how to control the minds of others and use the energies of others for selfish purposes. Individuals who use their powers in this direction in the unawakened state are called black magicians, as they consciously work with negative forces. They are not evil, simply unawakened to the higher life. There is no need to fear the work of such a person, for if you will be about the business of seeking more light,

THREE QUALITIES OF CONSCIOUSNESS AS REFLECTED IN HUMAN BEINGS

The three qualities are evident in nature and as man identifies with them he tends to exhibit certain behavior patterns.
1. Elevating Quality—That which tends to move toward the Center or which tends to resume the motionless state.
2. Activating Quality—Tends to remain stimulated and in motion.
3. Quality of Inertia—Tends toward manifestation on this plane, is the quality of heaviness and dense consciousness.

In Relationship to:	Elevating Quality Manifesting	Activating Quality Manifesting	Quality of Inertia Manifesting
Movement	Toward Reality Light, Bliss, etc.	Caught up in activity. Semi-light.	Apathetic Unknowing.
Choice of Food	Desires food that is pleasant to taste, wholesome.	Desires food that is heavily seasoned and irritating.	Eats lifeless food.
Mode of Worship	Worships celestial beings, then goes beyond form.	Concentrates on the low astral and psychic levels.	Nature Spirits if anything.
Speech	Reflects the positive mental attitude.	Meaningless, time wasting, etc.	Negative attitude. Crude.
Giving	Gives freely because of realization of contact with never ending supply.	Gives with reservation. Selfish consideration.	Gives with no consciousness of right time or place.
Realization	Has the vision of Reality; formless and in form.	Sees through the eyes of duality. Manifest forms.	Strictly materialistic.
Expression	Moves intuitively. Unmoved by the appearance world.	Is motivated by the pleasure-pain pattern.	Deluded. Inharmonious.

Most people are manifesting a combination of these qualities with certain obvious patterns predominating. All self discipline is aimed at helping the individual to get aligned with the desirable quality. The desirable quality being the elevating one, for this will insure rapid increase in awareness.

you will not be in attunement with their work, and therefore not influenced.

B. In the case of people who are manifesting the activating quality, we see an interest in using the mental powers, mostly as a diversion from the task of self-discipline which leads to enlightenment. At this stage many people will justify their work with the powers by saying that they are helping people, either by healing them or by helping them overcome personal problems. Often we see these people working for others even when they are not asked to work, thus their work becomes meddling in private affairs, rather than spiritual work. Even when they work on request and perform feats of mental magic, without really helping the person to help himself, they are still practicing sorcery, though this thought is not at all attractive to such a practitioner. Surprising as it may seem, even the effort to perform good works can be a form of bondage if one does not see the overall picture.

Of course, the individual who is manifesting the elevating quality will work with the powers in the highest manner, and this is the true Adept.

47. The Glorification or Perfection of the Body Is the Result of Supreme Realization Coupled with the Desire to Operate on This Plane.

When the eight powers are active in a pure state, the result is manifest in a perfected body. When every bit of darkness is refined from the body and there is purification on all levels, the perfect or glorified body is the instrument of operation on this plane. Naturally since the soul consciousness is supreme, the body which acts as the vehicle is refined due to contact with it. There is perfect function, normal balance in every part, and even a radiance given off due to the intense activity of the vital force within. Such a perfected body is not the result of diet, exercise or subconscious conditioning. It is the result of the illumined soul consciousness pervading the body.

48. Through Contemplation on the Nature and Purpose of the Body Organs Comes Mastery of the Body.

Again we are brought to the point that when illumination reaches into every part of the body, on all levels, then everything is revealed. With this revelation comes mastery. A Master is a master of his nature.

49. From Such Mastery Comes a Raising of the Vibration of the Body as the Body Converts into Mind-stuff and Complete Conquest of Nature, with or without a Body.

As the consciousness is purified (relieved of conditionings) then this is evident in the body as the vibrations are raised and the body lifted to a higher state. The body is really an extension of the mind, and the body as a whole is a solidified thought. Understanding this, it is natural to see that the body tends to take on the nature of light as the consciousness is illumined.

Also, at this stage of unfoldment there comes the permanent realization that it is no longer necessary to depend upon the mind action to know anything, and that the best way to know anything is simply to *know*. Direct perception or intuitive perception is the faculty of the soul. As long as the soul maintains contact with the body, there will be a flow of energies through the body, but only as a result of the contact, and not by necessity.

50. By Contemplating on the Nature of Soul and Spirit There Arises Realization of Omnipotence and Omnipresence.

The natural result of experiencing the illumination of consciousness is that the soul becomes fully aware of its full potential. This includes the awareness of omnipotence and omnipresence as well as all of the powers mentioned earlier.

Complete Liberation

51. By Renouncing Even the Attachment to Psychic Powers Comes Liberation of Consciousness.

As it is possible to become so fascinated by the display of powers that the goal of liberation can be overlooked, it is wise to remember to keep everything in its place. As long as the use of any ability is coupled with personal desire and an emotional coloring, there is still the possibility of remaining entangled in a web of psychic activity. While a liberated person could use these powers, he would still realize that they were not really necessary for existence. The liberated consciousness is *aware of awareness,* and does not need evidence to support its reality.

52. There Should Be No Compulsive Reaction to the Allurements or Attentions of Anyone on Any Level.

The path of illumination is a singular path and one must be willing to continue with or without the encouragement of others. It is a relationship between soul and Spirit and is entirely impersonal. For a person to be looking for attention, recognition or praise from anyone, and

Perfect Superconsciousness and Soul Ability

to use this as a mark of progress, is a failing. There are many levels of subtle activity and we can become aware of them as we unfold. Even when we are sure that we have mastered our reactions to what people on this plane can offer, there is still the possibility of being contacted by individuals from other worlds (planes and dimensions) as our awareness increases. Often our relationship with such individuals is much the same as our relationship with men and women on this plane. We are subject to the same subtle forms of flattery, enticement and even criticism. There is a tendency for many people to feel, surely they are in tune with celestial realms if they earn the attention of beings in light bodies, and to feel that they must listen to the advice of such beings. Remember, as long as a soul is embodied, there is still the possibility that the desire pattern which allows him to have contact with a body, can also delude him. Do not make the mistake in assuming that just because a soul operates a body of different vibration from you that he is necessarily possessed of clearer vision. There are many levels of consciousness even in the realms of light.

53. Intuitive Knowledge of the Fourth Dimensional Concept as a Result of Contemplation on Particles of Time.

It must be remembered that in the cosmic sense, everything is contained in the totality of being; yet when this totality of being is viewed from a certain level, it appears that there is multiplicity of form and a great variety of activity taking place. Our acceptance of this and our understanding due to a limited viewpoint, constitutes illusion. Man remains confused as long as he does not see the whole picture, but when the veil lifts, *he sees every-*

thing in its proper place and comprehends the fourth dimensional concept, which is the fact that all levels of consciousness, all points of view, all experiences, exist in the ever-present now, and that man experiences a passage of time because his attention shifts from one level of consciousness to another, from one point of view to another, and from one experience to another. It is not that time passes, but man's attention moves from point to point.

Understanding this, we come to the realization that as far as we are concerned as individuals, we do not have to wait for any experience to come to us; *we have but to identify with it as it exists in the now.* Our ability to accept it as being our personal experience is the key to easy expression in this world. Many people try for years to make something happen, without realizing that everything is *happening* right now in the true sense. Life is *being* what it has always been, right now. There never was a time when Life was not being Itself. We are of necessity dealing with individual experience. As far as you are concerned as an individual, there is no reason why you cannot move into the realization of the cosmic consciousness in this incarnation. There is no need to postulate a succession of incarnations as a prerequisite for this to happen.

By using the technique of contemplation—that is, by directing the flow of attention to the mystery of time, the confusion of the subject will be released and the fourth dimensional reality will dawn. Just as objects seem to be situated in position in this three dimensional reality, so in the fourth dimensional reality, the points of view, levels of consciousness, and experiences realized by people, exist and need only to be contacted. To contact an experience which seems beyond your grasp, try releasing a

Perfect Superconsciousness and Soul Ability 127

present experience which seems to be in conflict with the one desired.

Time sense is also related to movement, based upon the movement of the smallest particle of matter. The mass acceptance of the passage of time makes it possible for human beings to plan for the future, and remember the past. A true understanding of this time sense makes it possible for a person to transcend it, and thereby see past, present and future, as one. From this vantage point, when desire patterns of individuals or groups of individuals are known through intuition, it can be predicted what they will experience, or identify with, in the future, if they do not change existing patterns. This is not a process of looking into the future, but of seeing the trend from present indications.

Realization of the fourth dimensional concept gives the view of a world which is even more solid and more real, in this sense, than the three dimensional viewpoint can give. Instead of losing contact with reality as we cognize the various dimensions, we become more securely anchored *in Reality,* for we are extending the awareness to realize the whole.

54. **Because of the Unfoldment Which Is the Natural Result of Steady Contemplation on the Nature of Manifest Life, There Comes a Realization of All Life Forms, Their Nature, Quality and Place in the Scheme of Things.**

When man has partial illumination he comprehends to a degree, the energies and forces of nature, but since he does not see the whole picture, he confuses the issue and introduces error into his philosophy of life. When we work from the top down, there is full realization of the activities of the One Life as it steps down in frequency and manifests on various planes. There are connecting rays of light between every manifestation of this plane and beyond, for nothing exists of itself.

55. Realization of the Absolute Gives Peace Because It Reveals Truth.

When the ultimate truth is realized, there is perfect peace. This peace must not be confused with the attitude of smugness which is to be seen in people who *think* they have the truth, for it is not a mental attitude at all, but a knowingness.

56. When the Soul Aligns the Actions with the Elevating Quality and Moves in Harmony with the Spirit, Then Liberation Is Attained.

An Adept functions with full awareness of Spirit. With or without a body, the consciousness remains undimmed, for then the body is seen as an extension of the mind, and a tool for contact with the plane upon which the Adept is working at the time. The body is in harmony with the elevating qualities of nature and everything is geared to the universal economy; therefore the Adept lives as a liberated soul. Even if he should perform actions which were judged by others of limited vision to be inconsistent with truth, if the judgment were due to ignorance, no bondage to action is engendered. A liberated Adept has no concept of right and wrong, good and bad, success or failure, in the ordinary sense, but moves in harmony with Life, freely and without restriction. Even in the world, he is not of it. Being a pure soul, there is nothing that can touch him. He realizes his true nature

Perfect Superconsciousness and Soul Ability

at all times. He does not live in the past, but in the ever-present now. Reincarnation is no more for him, though he might appear to die and reincarnate. To him it is still an experience of Being, for as the ordinary man in an objective frame of mind is aware of the nothingness of his dream experiences, they being manifest from subconscious records and impressions, so the Adept sees this world and all levels of manifest creation as a dream. He can live in it, but he sees through it, and since he sees through it, there is no bondage.

This is perhaps one of the most difficult things to understand for the average student, because everyone is used to judging from appearances and from personal standards, failing to realize that such standards are only relative and usually imposed as a convenience. Also, due to much misinformation which has been written over the years by well-meaning but unrealized people, we are often led to believe that an Adept must appear as characterized—always benign, always forgiving, always otherworldly. It comes as quite a shock to find an Adept who is practical, who insists upon adherence to cosmic law, and who is very much *in* this world for the time he has chosen to reside here. Students do themselves a disservice by trying to find an Adept made in their image. It is still true that the only way to really understand an Adept is to attain his state of consciousness and see life through his eyes.

BOOK FOUR

Liberation

LIBERATION

1. The Psychic Powers Are Attained by Birth, Chemical Means, Use of Sound, Asceticism or Concentration.

In the last chapter we discussed the eight major powers which come as a result of awakening. There are some people who have natural ability in one area or another because they carry it over from a previous incarnation. Abilities attained in one incarnation, if used, will appear automatically in the following incarnations. This accounts for the natural ability of some people to see auras, exercise mental telepathy, and feel an urge to unfold. There are many methods used to attain the use of the powers. Among them are:

A. *The Use of Chemicals.* By using chemicals, usually taken through the mouth, it is possible to depress certain brain centers and excite the psychic energies to such an extent that an extended awareness is forced upon a person. For centuries, individuals who lacked the ability to use the powers at will, have taken chemicals into the body, and in this way have experienced various stages of mystical trance, visions, and release from the bondage of the body and body patterns. This experience is brief, of course, but it does show that the ability to extend the awareness is latent in all of us and is simply a matter of getting free from present conditionings.

The use of chemicals for attaining liberation is not recommended for several reasons. One reason is that forcing the psychic nature to manifest without a corresponding elevation in the quality of consciousness will simply open more doors to greater areas of confusion. Lacking the objectivity to handle the reservoir of desire patterns and subconscious tendencies, which are brought to the surface when the conscious mind is broken through, will tend to unbalance the individual, as he finds his world being flooded with a debris of mental pictures and emotional memories over which he has no control. Another reason for not using this means to break into the greater awareness, is the danger of becoming dependent upon the use of the drug in question, either as it alters the chemical balance in the body, or as the mind accepts it as the easy way to inner experience and forgets that the drug is unnecessary. The use of drugs to open the door of memory for the purpose of therapy, of course, is to be recommended.

B. *The Use of Sound.* By the proper use of audible affirmation, leading to silent work and contemplation on the cosmic sound (see techniques), the inner activity is encouraged. The pure-minded aspirant will use only the technique of merging with the cosmic sound as his approach. Here we will note that it is possible through the use of sound and the use of chants, to control certain elements. This is a lower method of operation and is not even considered by sincere students.

C. *Unfoldment Through the Practice of Asceticism.* In this sense, asceticism does not mean self-punishment or self-denial for the purpose of righting a supposed wrong. Self-punishment springs from a psychological need to be punished and is a perversion of asceticism. What is the basis for asceticism? It is this: When a balanced, healthy-minded individual cuts himself off from contact with this world, and the mind is not being fed with a stream of impressions, the natural reaction is to

Liberation

experience confusion because the familiar points of orientation are missing. The average person finds contentment in the fact that he knows where he is, and how he fits into his pattern of living. He grows accustomed to living with other people and in seeing the world as it appears to be. He may be normal in the sense that he is in harmony with mass agreements, but as far as realizing his soul nature is concerned, he may be resting in almost total ignorance.

Now when the average person experiences a cut-off from his environment, his first reaction is to remember how it was and try to preserve his balance with the memory. But, as the impressions cease to flow in to confirm his memory, he begins to doubt the reality of his memory and, lacking orientation points, begins to experience a breaking up of his stable mental pattern. If the person is lacking in even the basic understanding of what life is all about and has no understanding of the nature of soul perception, and if he thinks he has to operate through a body and mind, he tends to become confused. The probability is that the person will become neurotic and eventually psychotic. This is seen all over the world when people are forced to change their viewpoints without understanding what is going on. As long as a person holds to a viewpoint as reality, he will be constantly shaken as he moves from viewpoint to viewpoint, but if he comes to the realization that he is a soul and that he can embrace any viewpoint at will, then he will be stable and in good shape. This is why it is valuable to learn the basic principles and strike a mental and emotional balance before trying to unfold through meditation, or any other way. This is also the reason for the failure of people who try to find liberation through any route except meditation, because when they force open the door of the psychic world, they cannot cope with what they find. And the type of person who is desperate enough to use these other methods is not usually aware enough to take responsibility for what happens.

For a person who is balanced, periods of seclusion are helpful and brings good results. The purpose of asceticism is this: By cutting off the contact with the outside world, and by renouncing everything that is not the unmanifest consciousness, the unmanifest state or pure consciousness is revealed. *Regardless of what looms before the inner vision, the true practitioner of this science strikes it aside with the knowledge that it is illusory in nature and not the eternal Reality.*

Periods of asceticism can best be practiced from time to time. There is no virtue to a life of self-denial, for it proves nothing except lack of understanding. It is possible to live a full life in this world and still maintain a complete understanding on all levels. To refuse to eat certain foods, to refuse to communicate with people, to refuse to enjoy life, is not a spiritual way to live. Fellowship, a life of intense activity, and the assuming of great responsibility, on the other hand, cannot take the place of self-knowledge. There must be balance on all levels.

D. *Concentration as a Way to the Attainment of the Powers.* The best way to come into realization of the powers, is through balanced meditation and observance of the rules to be found in detail in Part II of this book. It will insure balanced unfoldment every step of the way.

2. **The Result of the Elevation of Consciousness Is That the Body Operated by the Soul Is Transformed in Keeping with the New Level of Consciousness.**

As the body is a manifestation of consciousness, it stands to reason that as the consciousness changes, the

Liberation 137

body will change. The body of an Adept, for instance, may appear to be of the same nature as an ordinary body, but it is devoid of impurities and actually vibrates at a different level. This is due to the action of pure consciousness filtering through the layers of consciousness known as mental, astral and physical bodies. As it is true for the individual, so it is true for the race, and in the distant future when the mass mind is illumined, there will be no comparison between the bodies now being used. In form they will be similar, but in density they will be different. The nervous system will be refined and even new areas opened to permit the passage of lifetronic forces which at present cannot flow except in the refined bodies of awakened souls. This takes place over a period of time in the masses, but can be facilitated in the individual who will take conscious part in the process and practice working with the available techniques, such as working with the light, and merging in the cosmic sound.

3. **The Practice of the Techniques Is Not the Cause of the Increase in Awareness, but They Act as a Means of Removing the Obstacles of the Free Flow of Consciousness.**

This is a very subtle point and a disappointment to many sincere students. The practice of the techniques will not in themselves insure the illumination of consciousness. They cannot make anything happen, because in the true sense the ultimate level of consciousness is available right now. All they can do is help remove the obstructions so that you can experience truth directly. Many persons are frustrated because they have faithfully practiced meditation as best they know how, and yet they have little or nothing to show for it. We must remember that we are not developing and we are not growing in the true sense, but we are removing the obstructions so that we may perceive truth.

As we practice emotional and mental control, correct posture for meditation, life force control, interiorization of the mental faculties, concentration, meditation and absorption, we put our house in order and make ourselves receptive to the inflow of power and the recognition of the Absolute.

4. Egoism Is the Cause of the Individualization of Cosmic Mind.

Though we talk of One Mind, it is obvious that to a man of dual vision there are individualizations of this mind, until it seems that there are many independent minds. Egoism, or the sense of being separate from the larger ocean of mind, is the cause of this individualization. The question arises quite naturally, "Why the individualization of cosmic mind?" When the soul leaves the subjective omnipresence, it is to become enmeshed in matter by contacting the finer energies, thought forms, and finally matter. It is not to be assumed, however, that souls find themselves in contact with matter on this plane only or this planet only. There are numberless dimensions, teeming with life of all kinds, and the life forms in these dimensions have their own pattern of unfoldment. The average concept of the experience of the soul is entirely too small when compared with the reality of the thing.

Soul begins its attachment to matter usually with a small particle, and as it becomes Self-conscious, it identifies with more complex life forms so as to manifest its consciousness constructively, and so it moves, through the plants, simple life forms, and eventually to the hu-

Liberation

man body. In the human body when the urge to extend the awareness continues, new and more refined areas are opened in the body so that the soul might find full expression. The unfoldment continues until consciousness transcends the body awareness, disconnects from the control centers, and functions through a more universal body.

5. In Spite of the Appearance of Diversity of Forms, There Is But One Reality. Consciousness, the Eternal Reality, Appears as Form.

This basic truth should be remembered at all times, even in the midst of the most exacting activities. Since all problems follow the acceptance of a dual creation, it stands to reason that if the concept of oneness is maintained, this understanding will liberate the mind. Too many, otherwise sincere students, fluctuate in their stand for principle.

6. Among the Various Levels of Consciousness, Only That Level Attained in Perfect Superconsciousness Is Free of Desire Patterns and Mental Forms.

In order for consciousness to manifest as form, *it must contain mental patterns equivalent to the appearance.* Within every manifest form, there are patterns, and intense activity, on all levels. As the soul intuitively identifies with these levels, it is aware of the inner and outer nature of that which it contemplates. Only when the soul is resting in the perfect superconscious state is it free of contact with desire patterns. The way to overcome desire and reaction patterns is to rise above them or come to the viewpoint of the recognition of the unmanifest state.

7. **While the Activities of Liberated Persons Are Free from Attachment, the Works of Ordinary Individuals Are Colored by the Three Qualities Found in Nature.**

Remember, in this chapter we are dealing with the perfected consciousness, and because of this we must draw our conclusions from this viewpoint. We have remarked at length that an Adept moves without compulsion and is always in the right place at the right time. Even when he appears to work and take part in the activities of this world, there is still a freedom of action and no sense of bondage, due to the perfect vision being maintained.

People on the ordinary levels of consciousness, however, experience according to the quality they allow to mingle with their actions. Individuals who cling to the destructive quality find their actions tinged with this quality and they suffer in the ordinary sense until they awaken from their ignorance. Persons who are restless, do work in this world but without a real sense of purpose and at the end of the line they find that they do not have the sense of satisfaction they thought they would have. They experience emptiness because their motives were not of the highest nature. Their creative expression keeps them busy while they are at it, but they often see their work turn to ashes right before their very eyes and see that life has been fruitless.

The awakened soul who is approaching liberation always works with a sense of purpose. This lays the groundwork for eventual self-realization and is an indication that illumination is near. This person works because it is his nature to be active; and as he makes a conscious effort to be an instrument for the flow of Power, he finds that he is lifted higher and higher in consciousness. The restless man, on the other hand, even though he tries to work constructively, is often so concerned with overcoming evil with good, that his obsession to do good works, blinds him to the extent that he remains a victim of the dual vision. As long as there is compulsive desire there is bondage, for compulsion indicates reaction, and reaction indicates a belief in the reality of the appearance world. While the world of appearance is real, it has no separate existence and could not exist without the Whole.

This doctrine of transcending the karmic law is one of the most difficult to understand for many people because they have been conditioned for so many years that they have to pay for their mistakes and must atone for their transgressions. This is so stressed that people tend to develop a guilty conscience, and their low opinion of self brings on the pain and punishment. When you come to the realization of who you really are, you open to the awareness of the Eternal-Now, and this automatically frees you from anything you think you did in the past. The slate is wiped clean.

8. From the Karmic Patterns Are Projected the Body Form and Environment Required to Match the State of Consciousness Equal to the Understanding.

The body as we see it, and the physical environment, is the result of desires being fulfilled and dreams being materialized. What we see about us is the effect of a past series of decisions. Our personal affairs are in mathematical harmony with our desire patterns, for an unmodified desire always externalizes. We are born into a situation which fits our desire pattern, and experience a modification of consciousness accordingly.

Here we see the great mistake that many make, of assuming that they can live by grace and everything will turn out all right, without having been established in the perfect superconscious state. We contain within the astral and mental bodies, many layers of desire patterns, as yet unmanifest; and when we relax the conscious mind and just drift, without having realized the Absolute, these deep-seated patterns emerge and find expression. If the patterns which bring good fortune emerge, then we say that we are led of the Spirit; but if patterns which cause confusion emerge, then we say that we are being punished or taught a lesson. This is ignorance of the worst sort and is really a sign of spiritual laziness.

Many desire patterns are carried from incarnation to incarnation until a situation is confronted which will release them and bring about their fulfillment. These patterns can be neutralized as we fall in line with constructive activity, they can be modified as we put in motion desire patterns which cancel them, or they can be erased by the cosmic fire in joyous meditation. Especially does this happen in the practice of kriya, for the passing of the life current through the spine and brain works directly on the deep-seated tracings which are filed in that area.

Just as a shadow is cast automatically when a pattern is held before a light, so human experience is the result of these mental patterns being held before the ever-flowing ocean of substance.

9. Even Though Desire Patterns Appear to Work Out with a Lack of Order, Still There Is Order and Patterns Externalize Steadily, Even Though It Appears That They Are Disconnected by Time and Space. As Self-knowledge Dawns There Comes Also a Memory of How This Takes Place.

It may be that even if there is a chain of desire patterns awaiting fulfillment, they will externalize a few at a time, rather than in a continuous experience. This is due to the fact that they must externalize in an environment that is in harmony with the manifestation. At times there is a period of several years or even several incarnations between experiences of a similar nature, so it is obvious that the chain of experience is broken by time and space. This accounts for a streak of good fortune that comes for no apparent reason and a streak of ill fortune that comes in the same way. At times these things happen and there can be no direct connection found with present time thoughts or feelings.

This need not frighten a true student. When negative patterns begin to externalize, then adjust your viewpoint so that you are aware of the truth of your being, that you are a free soul, and you will neutralize the effects of past decisions and compulsive desires. We need not be a slave to the past. One of the beautiful things about this science is that everything can be confirmed through meditation. When the inner vision opens, the knowledge of these chains of desire is revealed; and as it happens, there is an unravelling of the past, which is nothing more than recorded patterns existing in the present.

10. As the Urge for Expression Is Inherent in the Spirit, Desire Is Impersonal and Has No Origin.

Spirit is manifest and yet, remains unmanifest. The manifest being the extension of the unmanifest and can be drawn back at any time without loss or harm. The ocean can contain pieces of ice or it can be free of ice; it still remains the same substance. Nothing is lost; only the form has ceased to be. Spirit does not remain static for long, for there is always a pulsing taking place, a sending out and a drawing back. This urge to express takes form in man as desire, but in the average man this desire is impure; that is, it is colored by the quality of nature, according to man's understanding. Because of this, man being the individualization of Spirit, experiences confusion and takes time to regain his awareness. The urging is impersonal. It is impossible for a man to remain in a body and not have desire; and as long as man recognizes the nature of desire, that it is the impersonal action of Spirit, there is no bondage.

We say that desire has no origin because Spirit has no origin, and desire is necessary in Spirit, before Spirit can take form. Misunderstanding on this point has caused much suffering, as well-meaning people have tried to cut off all desire and feeling, and instead of realizing cosmic consciousness they create a static condition and are very unhappy. There is a method of attaining liberation by feeling the flow of the Spirit through the senses and by recognizing the Spirit as the stuff of this world. This viewpoint makes for radiant living and true happiness. It is possible when we come to the realization, that indeed, this world is the manifestation of Spirit, or when we affirm that there is but consciousness and consciousness

Liberation

in form. We see that it is a matter of recognition instead of self-denial.

11. **Form Is Held in Time and Space by the Steady Maintenance of the Mental Pattern, and When the Mental Pattern Is Released, the Energies, Life Forces, and Light Particles Are Disbursed.**

Here we find the secret of creation and the answer to dissolving any situation which seems to be undesirable in the present. We again refer to the realm of mental images, through which the ever-flowing substance flows, to appear on this level. A body, a form of any kind, proves the existence of a desire, either conscious or unconscious. Controlled creation is desirable, for at least when this is the rule, we have dominion. The average person will not take responsibility for his present life situation, and because of this he is powerless to change it. *To change a situation one must assume responsibility for it and then create a situation to take its place.*

An Adept does not concern himself with controlling energies and mental forces through visualization, or use of affirmation, or by dominating specific individuals. An Adept works from a high level of consciousness and simply *wills* a situation to be so, and lets it manifest through the individuals who are willing to be instruments for the flow. Thus everyone is benefited and Life acts upon Itself in infinite harmony. An Adept does not *use* the Consciousness, but merely frames the pattern by making a decision that a certain situation will be, or that a certain thing will manifest. *I must stress the impersonal operation of the law, for the Spirit will work through any and all instruments who are willing.*

Things are held in form for just as long as the pattern

behind the thing is fed with attention. When the attention wanders, then the pattern is distorted or dissolved and the form on this level either distorts or vanishes from view. *This is the secret of solving problems.* Just take the attention from the pattern or belief which is supporting the problem, and flow the attention to the pattern which would imply the solution. It is really very simple, and that is why I stress *controlled* creation, or conscious understanding of what is taking place. When we understand the relationship between the subtle mental world and the apparent solid world, we will have the ability to precipitate matter.

12-13. The Form Which Exists in Time and Space Contains Also the Potential of Exhibiting New Characteristics, Shaded by the Qualities of Nature.

Because of the deep-seated, unmanifest desire patterns existing on subtle levels in the form, be it body of human, animal or plant, there also exists the possibility of these desire patterns rising to the surface when the occasion is ripe. As they do, the form may exhibit new characteristics and these characteristics will be shaded by the quality of consciousness which is dominant at the time. This explains the reason for negative characteristics developing for no apparent reason. The real understanding concerning any form should be that the perfect pattern is there, and it can emerge and remain manifest if it is concentrated upon. Regardless of the distortions of desire and aberration, the perfect pattern *can* come to the surface and be stabilized if it is recognized.

14. Motion Is Seen in the Rhythmic Activity of Nature.

When the eye of intuition opens we see balance and harmony in this world, where before we saw chaos and confusion. Behind the scenes there is a law of mind in action and everything is moving along according to a cosmic activity. There is a law in operation at all times which projects the appearance of form on the screen of time and space. Behind the appearance world we view a fantastic play of lights and shadows; and seeing the secret of creation, we are released from the concept of illusion forever.

15. Since Perceptions Concerning Objects Vary Between Individuals, It Is Obvious That Mind Is Deluded Concerning the Reality of Form.

There is a debate between different schools concerning the perception of form. Some will say that nothing exists until there is someone to be aware of it, as though their being aware of it, created it. In order for creation to have some semblance of stability, it must be frozen into form by mass perception. The agreed upon universe is the result of universal agreement and an individual may be able to cease to perceive it by an act of will, but it will still exist for those who can see it. At this point, we come to an interesting sidelight and it is this: *when we create a situation by an act of will, we usually forget how we did it, and accept the fact that it has independent reality.* This is why most people on this plane have such a hard time extending themselves beyond the level of mass agreement. They accept the reality of this world of form and fail to see beneath the surface.

Although we see form in this world pretty much the same, there is a little variance in our perception of it, springing partly from the fact that we tend to see through conditioned perceptions. We view a distorted picture, because our inner beliefs modify what we are really seeing. While it is true that consciousness manifesting in form is extending from the unmanifest level and is held in place by belief, on the universal level it is due to universal belief. It is conceivable that if a person would stand quietly and release himself from his accepted viewpoints, he would vanish from this world, though he would be real to himself and real to others who shared his level of understanding. This is how the Adepts travel from point to point in space. *By releasing the hold on one location and accepting another location as real, there is an instantaneous transfer of body from point to point or from dimension to dimension.*

This is also the secret of miracles performed by the man of pure vision. *Regardless of the condition experienced by the person in the belief of duality, if a pure-minded man decided to change the conditions, he could do it, simply by contacting it with his attention, then changing his acceptance of it. If a condition, now distorted, is contacted in consciousness by an Adept, it then becomes a part of his mindstuff; and since it is mirrored by his mind, he can change the reflection by changing his believing.* Thus we see healings of body and mind. It is not a departure from natural law, but an operation of the law from a deeper understanding.

16-17. The Forms Are Known or Unknown by Individualized Mind Depending upon Whether or Not There Is Conscious Identification, but the Levels of Mind Are Always Known in the Cosmic Sense.

When a person rests in the consciousness of being an individual, there are known factors in this world and unknown factors, depending upon whether there is any conscious identification of factors and form by the mind. That is, if one perceives a form, then it exists for him—otherwise it does not.

However, in the cosmic conscious experience it is possible to be aware of all levels of mind, since there is only one mind with various levels. Even though one may not always be aware of every conceivable form which has been manifest through the action of mind, he can still be conscious of the sea of mind in which everything is manifest. The entire range of mental activity makes up the cosmic mind, thus even the most minute activity of mind is still an example of cosmic mind in action, for there is no part of cosmic mind separated from the Whole.

18. Since the Mind Is Perceived, It Is Not the Ultimate Reality and Is Not the Source of Illumination.

As we have seen, the mind is an instrument, and a very convenient one at that, but it can be dissected and even transcended. It is not the individualized mind that knows anything, but Truth filters through the mind and is revealed. It is a mistake to assume that illumination comes from building the mind, for in the first place, the mind is not the source of illumination; and even when it is trained to be a perfectly operating instrument, it is still the product of conditioning. It is good to condition and discipline the mind, but at the same time be aware of the fact that it is a step to self-awareness which transcends mental activity. Too many people confuse intellectualism with illumination of consciousness. A person with a well disciplined mind and a vast store of data on hand is undoubtedly well equipped to operate in this world, but he can still remain ignorant of the ultimate Reality.

In deep meditation a point is reached where one can intuitively be aware of the mental activity. When you come to the realization that you are observing the mental activity, you have the understanding of being aware of awareness and that you are really something more than body and mind. This brings us to our statement at the head of this thought: "Since the mind is perceived, it is not the ultimate Reality and is not the source of illumination."

Illumination is experienced when all mental activity is eradicated and the conscious awareness is maintained. We do not have to build consciousness; we have but to come to the realization of the unconditioned or modified state.

19-20. The Mind Has No Power in Itself to Know Itself, and the Effort to Cognize Another Mind Leads to Confusion.

Since the individualized mind is really but a modification of universal mind, it has no separate reality. Therefore, the attempt of the mind to know itself leads to confusion. Sincere students often predicate the existence of other minds, and this also leads to never-ending conjecture. There is but one mind in the highest sense, and everything else that appears as individualized mind is a modification of this one mind. Even the universal mind is the instrument for the flow of power from the absolute center and is an object, and has no independent reality. As the universal mind is the instrument through which the Ultimate Reality works, so the individualized mind is the instrument of soul, which is a unit of the Ultimate Reality.

The mind, the mental body, the astral body or the physical body has not the power of independent awareness. The soul, identifying with these bodies, and with feeling and desire, thinks itself to be separate, but this is delusion. There are many life units identified with the body parts, but they fall in line with the overall body pattern and soul destiny. When you realize that you are soul, then you can detach yourself and *will* the mind to be in perfect order and it will be so. It is just a matter of the proper arrangement of electrical patterns.

21. **Unmodified Consciousness Becomes Self-conscious to the Degree That It Identifies with Form or Creation.**

Unmodified consciousness involves into matter by a gradual process of becoming more and more involved in the sea of desire patterns, feeling patterns and energy flows. The natural tendency is to identify with whatever is concentrated upon. As this is the secret of understanding involution, it is also the secret of attaining liberation. By contemplating the unmodified state it emerges to the surface once again. It is a simple thing in essence but the simplicity of it baffles many intelligent men and women. Just remember, "man becomes what he dwells upon," and you will never want for knowledge.

In the unmodified state which lies at the center of life, there is neither darkness nor light, feeling nor non-feeling, being nor non-being; there is only Reality. Since this is hard to comprehend by a mind that is used to having something to cognize, it is often only accepted as a philosophical viewpoint. Also, since the mind loves to be stimulated and entertained, it eyes with fear the possibility of being annihilated. Man finds it hard to accept the idea that he would be happy in this pure unmodified state, as he thinks it would be a state of nothingness. This is because he has been used to associating with forms for so long. He fails to grasp that it would be an experience of Totality, rather than a negative destruction of self. Because of this, many beautifully realized souls remain for mellenniums, at the edge of the ocean of Truth. These are the shining ones, who manifest in form and are the purest examples of what it is like to move in a consciousness of Light.

22. Being Acted upon by the World of Form and by the Ocean of Light, the Mind Reflects Illumination.

When we discuss the illumined mind, we are talking of the mind that has come to the point where it can accept the flood of truth and light and yet retain some conditioning and reality. At this time, there is a working of the light through the mind, into the world of form, as the mind acts as a transmitter of this underlying power. When the proper balance is struck, we see a working back and forth of this Power. The perfect interchange is symbolized by the interlaced triangles, the realm of light in harmony with the world of form—*Power descending, creation ascending.* A person in whom this condition is fully active is an Avatar.*

At this point the conditioned mind acts as the meeting place for the higher and lower levels of consciousness, and the soul wills the mind to retain certain modifications in order to retain its existence. The modified mind in this case is not held together by compulsive patterns of desire and feeling, but by *desireless* desires, which are radiations of the pure urge to manifest for a while on one plane or another. Such an incarnation is a consciously controlled experience; and when the individual desires to leave this plane, he accomplishes it simply by wiping out the mental patterns which are extending into this dimension as the body form. Thus the body either fades from view instantaneously or gradually falls apart and the

* Sanskrit word signifying Spirit fully manifested in the flesh body.

Spirit leaves it. A soul with this level of awareness also has the ability to create a body at will and bring it into phase with any dimension and then release it, by releasing the will that holds it in form.

23. **The Universal Substance Reflecting an Infinite Number of Individualized Mind Impressions Is Life Acting upon Itself and Affords Opportunity for the Soul to Extricate Itself in the Harmonious Process.**

As we are aware by now, the cosmic mental activity is the sum total of the collective mental activities—cosmic mind manifesting in infinite variety. When we have the non-dual vision, we see this whole thing as a cosmic manifestation, and our task is to unravel the mystery by attaining self-awareness. Because there is a law of balance in the harmonious working of this cosmic activity, the soul can depend upon basic principles to hold true and never deviate even a little. *This opportunity to depend upon the reliability of cosmic law gives a sense of security which is necessary for steady unfoldment. It is never a matter of dependence upon a person or situation, but upon an inflexible and never-yielding law.*

24. **Discrimination Between the Soul and Mind Brings the Realization That the Soul Is a Unit of Awareness Not Identified with Mind in Truth.**

This should be cause for great relief. As soul, you are that pure, untouched unit of awareness. *You were never confused, never involved, never made a mistake, can never be held accountable for anything. The soul does not learn lessons, for to assume this would be to classify it in the category of the mind.* The mind can be disciplined, controlled, modified. It can learn, and it can be unlearned or confused with incorrect data. The soul can never be confused or modified. *But when it identifies with the mind, it then loses this realization and the mind is dominant.*

Tremendous loads of guilt, regret and fear, can be dropped immediately when the realization of the soul nature is experienced. *All the concepts concerning karma and all the ideas concerning religious philosophy and human conduct go by the wayside.* Up to this point, rules and beliefs were an essential part of the process, for they enabled the mind to keep in the right direction until the soul consciousness emerged. But once the soul nature has fully come to the surface and governs the body and all the affairs, there arises a natural realization of the nature of Life. Then we understand, there is no power to be invoked, no level to attain, nothing to overcome, nothing to reject. *When we come to this glorious point of recognition, we cast aside all concepts and merge joyously in the ocean of Life.* We see that it is just as good to live on this plane as on any other, for the previously accepted barriers do not exist, as they have been stricken from the mind, which was the only place they had any reality in the first place. It is a tremendous thing to actually see the truth that as the inner barriers melt away—since the world is a reflection of the mind—they cease to exist in the environment. *This is the real significance of overcoming this world.*

It is also an overcoming of the concept of death. When we are moving in the fullness of consciousness, there is no dimming of our awareness; hence wherever we are, we are conscious of Life being what It is. Though we move through a succession of bodies, and a chain of experiences, we always retain our inner vision. We are al-

Liberation

ways the same, in the unshakeable realization of Cosmic Consciousness.

25. Intent upon the Vision of the Absolute, There Is the Tendency to Rise Above Identification with Mind and Form.

It seems that without a sense of purpose, a reason for being, a person who realizes the unmodified state gradually breaks contact with this world. The pull to the center seems to get stronger and stronger. This is the reason why most Adepts eventually leave their physical form, sometimes at an early age, because the pull is so strong and their desire for this plane is so weak. They almost always leave behind trained disciples, who are ready for the experience of illumination in this incarnation, but who retain a few more desire patterns and experience a bit more delusion, in order to carry on the work set in motion by the Master. One by one, these disciples attain their own liberation, and the chain of souls keeps on, to more and more subtle realms of light and consciousness.

26. The Thoughts Which Arise as Obstructions to the Attainment of Pure Vision Spring from Impressions.

As we are in tune with this level of activity, even though we try to maintain our detachment, we are constantly open to a barrage of suggestion, directed to us by other people with excitable minds. These impressions sometimes find their mark, and by becoming lodged in the subconscious, they tend to stir up other thoughts by association. This is why, in deep meditation, it is helpful to cut off from the distractions of this world, so that the inflow of suggestion does not cause a new mental activity to arise and eclipse the vision of Reality. *It is the mental activity and the subsequent identification of the mind with the relative world that keeps man reminded of the sense of separation.*

27. The Way to Destroy These Thoughts Is to Treat Them the Same as Ignorance and Egoism (Part II:10). And That Is to Reduce Them to the Causal Level and Resolve Them.

Any form, or anything which appears to have independent reality, can be reduced to the causal level or the idea level, because behind every form there is the idea of it. Once you see the idea level and cease to believe in the reality of the form, then you can banish the idea of it, and as far as you are concerned, the form will vanish also. The sense of ego has its basis as an idea. Even the belief in ignorance is a projection of the mind based upon incorrect data. Thoughts, subtle though they may appear, are things which exist because of the pattern behind them. With practice, you see how everything is really a shadow, projected by the Light as it filters through the causal patterns. This is a high level of operation.

28. The Man Who Arrives at This Peak, Who Then Releases the Desire for Further Realization, Finds Himself Lost in the Immensity of Cosmic Consciousness and All It Implies.

Here we come to a very subtle truth. *After much effort to discipline the mind so that it will be a fit instrument; after many hours of practice of the various techniques in order to refine the physical body and purify it on all levels; after coming to the level of consciousness where the*

Liberation

body is seen as a shadow extension of the mind of light; then, we are to release any desire for more knowledge. The reason for this is simple when understood. As long as there is a sense of longing for a greater state of consciousness, there is the direct implication of a sense of separation, and this sense of separation is what keeps the barrier in place. We must not assume to release the desire before coming to this point in consciousness, however, for if we do, we find that lacking the tremendous upward pull due to long experience in this exalted state, we simply remain in our present confused condition. Many students who say that they are letting go of any desire for illumination are signing their own ticket to years of continuing ignorance. *We can only let go and be lifted into the ultimate perfection when we have already touched the shores of that realization through conscious experience.*

Only the man who is capable of experiencing the high states of superconsciousness (Samadhi) is safe in letting go of desire for continued unfoldment. At this point the desire changes from compulsion due to lack of fulfillment to an impulse to regain the fullness of consciousness. *At this point if the effort is removed, the union is automatic.*

29. From This Ultimate Realization Comes Release from Pain Due to Ignorance and the Necessity of Working with the Law of Reaction. (Karma)

When the last veil has been removed, there can be no more pain. The goal is at last attained. Remember, in the first pages of this work, it was stated that the goal of this mystic science was to remove the possibility of pain being experienced in the future? We have learned how to rest in the awareness of Self and be free of pain. Now that the goal of absolute realization has been attained, the possibility of pain ever being experienced in the future is banished forever, for the Light cannot retain any impressions of mind at this level. And without the retention of impressions there can be no reaction experienced. *Also from this level of consciousness, the soul sees how this consciousness makes things out of itself, by becoming the thing in question, and thus the mystery of creation is solved.* Realizing this truth, it becomes a matter of merely extending the consciousness to take form as desired, and withdrawing it when the form no longer serves a purpose. This is accomplished by extension and contraction, just as the cosmic mind extends the universes and draws them back into Itself. This is an impersonal activity and above the idea of entanglement in cause and effect. At this level the only cause, is the decision to manifest, and then the manifestation extends from the Center. At the time the desire for manifestation is released, the form takes the original unmodified state and no trace is left except on the ethers. This, too, is dissolved at the time of the dissolution of all form, when creation is withdrawn for a period into the bosom of the Absolute.

30. Realization of the Absolute, Without Impurities or Relative Forms, Gives Complete Understanding.

At this point the soul becomes Spirit. There is no sense of separation. Everything that we say the Spirit is, the soul becomes. This comes about eventually, but for most people it is a long process, in the sense of time. But it is a pleasant process, because once the superconscious state is reached, the sense of pain is overcome, and from then on it is a joyous experience. Souls operate through light bodies, then thought forms, for trillions of years, before merging completely.

31-33. The Ultimate Is Attained When the Qualities of Consciousness Are Dissolved, Then the Concepts of Time and Space, Ideas of Purpose and Significance Fade Away and the Soul Rests in Its True Nature.

Now when we come to the point where we dissolve the concept of body and mind and rest in consciousness, there remains only the resolution of these qualities from deadening, activating, to elevating, in that order, until the qualities are no more, in relationship to the soul. At this point the concept of space, which is tied in with time and helps give the consideration of dimensions and planes, is also resolved and the soul rests in the Totality of Being. This is Reality.

Center for Spiritual Awareness has world headquarters in northeast Georgia. *Here on a ten-acre site are found the spacious education building, administrative offices, residence homes, library and meditation temple. CSA is not a commune, nor is it a spiritual community in the usually accepted sense. It is a service center from which literature and training aids flow to a waiting world, and a retreat center to which seekers come for instruction and spiritual refreshment.*

If you would like informative literature about books, recordings and available programs, you have but to contact the CSA office. There is no obligation. We are here to serve you as you unfold your inborn divine potential. Contact: Center for Spiritual Awareness, Lake Rabun Road, Post Office Box 7, Lakemont, Georgia 30552.